Unveiling Paul's Women

Unveiling Paul's Women

Making Sense of 1 Corinthians 11:2–16

LUCY PEPPIATT

With a Foreword by Scot McKnight

CASCADE *Books* · Eugene, Oregon

UNVEILING PAUL'S WOMEN
Making Sense of 1 Corinthians 11:2–16

Cascade Books
An Imprint of Wipf and Stock Publishers
199 W. 8th Ave., Suite 3
Eugene, OR 97401

www.wipfandstock.com

PAPERBACK ISBN: 978-1-4982-8922-1
HARDCOVER ISBN: 978-1-4982-8924-5
EBOOK ISBN: 978-1-4982-8923-8

Cataloguing-in-Publication data:

Names: Peppiatt, Lucy | McKnight, Scot, foreword writer

Title: Book title : Unveiling Paul's women : making sense of 1 Corinthians
    11:2–16 / Lucy Peppiatt, with a foreword by Scot McKnight.

Description: Eugene, OR: Cascade Books, 2018 | Includes bibliographical refer-
    ences.

Identifiers: ISBN 978-1-4982-8922-1 (paperback) | ISBN 978-1-4982-8924-5
    (hardcover) | ISBN 978-1-4982-8923-8 (ebook)

Subjects: LCSH: Bible. Corinthians, 1st—Criticism, interpretation, etc. | Bible.
    Epistles of Paul—Criticism, interpretation, etc. | Women—Religious as-
    pects—Christianity | Equality—Biblical teaching

Classification: BS2675.52 P362 2018 (print) | BS2675.52 (ebook)

01/17/18

For Nick, my darling husband

Contents

Permissions

Foreword

Just in case you think an interpretation of Scripture can't be wrong early and stay wrong for centuries, think about Romans 16:7 and the story of Junia. She was a woman whose name was changed to Junias because, so it was believed, the person was an apostle and an apostle can't be a woman. So some males changed the woman into a man and, presto, we got a man named Junias. The problem is that there is no evidence for a male name "Junias" in the first century. The deed was done, and that's not our point: Junia remained Junias until, truth be told, the last quarter of the twentieth century when scholars realized the truth, admitted the mistaken history of interpretation, and acted on their convictions to restore the woman. Knocking off non-existent males is no moral problem, and raising a woman from the dead is a good thing. Junia is now inscribed in the best translations.

Sometimes our readings of the Bible are both mistaken and harmless: though many preachers during Advent can get worked up about whether or not Jesus was not given room in an "inn" or "guest room," the second translation will not affect many of us (Luke 2:7). Sometimes our readings may be mistaken and an improved, refined reading will convey deeper and more accurate truths. Studies now show that the word used by Paul in Romans 3:25, often translated "propitiation" (KJV), means "sacrifice of atonement" (NIV), and this improvement shifts the evocations of theology and atonement in the passage. One of the gifts of living in the twenty-first century is the accumulation of insights and improvements in our understanding of the Bible.

I'm persuaded that Lucy Peppiatt is pushing us to significant improvement when it comes to 1 Corinthians 11. The history of interpretation has had one angle: the women were the problem. But were they? What happens when we ask instead, as Lucy does with aplomb, if the *men* were the problem? Lots, that's what happens. Here's why we need to rethink how we read 1 Corinthians 11: that text says things about women that (1) are not like anything else in the whole Bible, (2) that are at odds with Paul's own theology, (3) that cut against the grain of Paul's own practice as seen in the Book of Acts, and (4) that create unbearable tension in 1 Corinthians itself.

When I first discovered Lucy's theory, and recalled seeing anything like it only one other time (and it impressed me, but I didn't have time to come to terms with the approach), what I most wanted was a printed version of 1 Corinthians 11:2–16 with the bits from Paul distinguished from the bits by those who were in tension with Paul's own teaching. I wanted to see it in a way that made the reading of it with his fresh approach compelling and simple. As with others, however, I also wanted a version of her argument for lay folks and non-specialists so more could see the beauty and simplicity and accuracy of her reading. We now have this in *Unveiling Paul's Women*.

Look, folks, there's been too much power of males used against women and when it is males, males, males making decisions on (1) what this passage means and (2) what women can do in churches, the early misreading of this text is simply multiplied and propagated and unchecked. It is time for us all to take a deep breath, take a step back, find a chair and a table for conversation, and rethink the traditional reading of this crucial and history-shaping passage in Paul. The irony of the traditional view is that, while there are hardly any agreements on what individual expressions and terms mean, there is one agreement: the women were the problem.

Not so.

Scot McKnight, Ph.D.
Julius R. Mantey Professor of New Testament
Northern Seminary, Lisle Illinois

Preface

Have you ever read 1 Corinthians 11:2–16 and wondered what Paul is going on about? I hope, if you have read it, that you *did* find it confusing. If you did, it means you were trying to think it through. Anyone who has really tried to get to the bottom of what Paul meant in this short passage has probably discovered that 1 Corinthians 11:2–16 is genuinely one of the most difficult biblical passages to understand. Even really clever and scholarly people are baffled by some of it. Tom (N. T.) Wright told me in a conversation that in his opinion this is the most difficult set of verses in the whole Bible! This passage confuses scholars and challenges preachers. Most ordinary men and women, who simply want to understand what the Bible means for them in everyday life, basically end up ignoring it.

In my book *Women and Worship at Corinth: Paul's Rhetorical Arguments in 1 Corinthians*, I explain how we might make sense of this difficult text along with two other tricky passages: 1 Corinthians 14:20–25 and 14:33–36. In the past few years, however, people have often asked me if I would write a shorter, simpler version of my academic book focusing only on 1 Corinthians 11:2–16 and the troubling question of head coverings for women. This is that book. It's like an extended Bible study on one passage and was written for people who want to gain an understanding of what Paul might have meant in 1 Corinthians 11:2–16, but is simpler in its approach. If you're interested in knowing the more complex details of the scholarly debates around this passage, and some of the background to 1 Corinthians as a letter, you should read *Women and Worship* as well. If you're simply interested in discovering what Paul meant when he talked about head coverings in 1 Corinthians 11, what that means for men and women today, and whether we should pay any attention to this in our churches, then read on.

Acknowledgments

This book would never have been written if I were not an academic who spends more of her time with the church than the academy. I'd like to thank my main church family, Crossnet, and my other community, WTC, for being places that constantly encourage me in my work, expand my thinking, and support me in what I do. I can't think of two more loving, Christ-like, and Spirit-filled communities, and I'm enormously grateful to the friends I have in both.

Thanks goes to those friends who have read and commented on a version of this book: Tina Cooke, Nick Crawley, Claire Fenner, Joshua Heslop, Scot McKnight, and Jo Pestell. Your discerning comments have made this a better book. The flaws remaining are my own!

I would also like to thank Robin Parry and Wipf and Stock Publishers. Robin's unstinting friendship and support has made so much possible that most certainly wouldn't have happened without him. I am hugely grateful for this. In addition to this, there is something about the people at Wipf and Stock that has deeply impressed me over the years. They know how to treat people like people. They are fun, courteous, and generous—qualities that matter. And most importantly for a publisher, they give people who might not otherwise have a voice, a place to speak. This is directly relevant to this work.

Special thanks go to Scot McKnight for encouraging me every step of the way. Scot's commitment to enabling and empowering women to reach their potential in the church, the academy, and the workplace is unflinching. He and Kris are wonderful and I'm privileged to call them friends.

Although I think he would be surprised to be mentioned in this book, I would like especially to thank Michael Lakey, a 1 Corinthians scholar and an Anglican priest, whose work has shaped my own more than anyone else's. He is the only Corinthians scholar I know of about whom I think if I am wrong, then he is right. In addition to this, as someone who openly disagrees with me, he has modeled an exceptional spirit of academic generosity and grace, and I have loved my engagements with him over the last year and a half. It gives me hope for the academy and the church.

I always want to thank my four sons for anything that gets written in my home. Although they've now finally all left, they continue to provide me with constant laughter, silliness, compassion, support, and even correction! They love ideas, Scripture, and theology, and they enrich our lives beyond words.

My final thanks go to my husband, Nick Crawley. I don't know anyone else who would have endless conversations about 1 Corinthians at 5am over a cup of tea. Everyone who knows us knows that I couldn't possibly do what I do without him. For him, and God's grace in Christ, I am eternally grateful.

Introduction

AN "AHA!" MOMENT

A few years ago, when I was studying 1 Corinthians, I had a thought that stopped me in my tracks. It was a revolutionary moment, and it proved to be a moment that would change the way I understood Paul on women forever.

"It was the men!" I said to my husband, as he walked through the door into my study. He looked a little bemused. "What do you mean, 'it was the men'?" "It was the men," I said, "who were the problem at Corinth. It wasn't the women at all. It was the *men.*" He looked at me, and then slowly sat down. He and I had both read a lot of commentaries on 1 Corinthians and he had studied the book over many years. I could see him computing what I'd just said.

He knew that I was thinking about the difficult passages about women in the letter because we'd been talking about them while I'd been studying 1 Corinthians. We'd been going over and over different ideas of what Paul might have meant. As I watched him thinking, I knew he was beginning to see what I thought I saw. What if it wasn't the women who were the problem in Corinth, but the men who were the problem after all? What if Paul was correcting the men? This moment was going to change the way we would read 1 Corinthians forever and this book will show you what we saw as a result. In addition to that, it wasn't just *one* of Paul's letters that took on a totally different meaning that day. So much of what we had already believed for so many years about the place of men and women in the church and even in the world began to fall into place in a much clearer way.

BEMUSED BY PAUL

I love Paul's writings. Some women hate him, and some women just avoid him, but I knew that I loved him. For years I brushed over the difficult passages on women, finding that everything else he said was life-giving, profound, and fascinating. I thought to myself, who could read Romans or Galatians or Ephesians without being touched by him as a man and a pastor? In my early days as a Christian I wasn't a scholar and I felt no real obligation to try and work out the difficult bits in Paul's writings. Later on I went into academic theology and found I couldn't really ignore the questions that people, and especially my own students, had about Paul. On top of that, I was a pastor in church leadership, and I had been appointed as the principal of a theological college. My "position" meant that I had to sort out what I thought the Bible really said about women in leadership. At the same time I realized that so many of *Paul's* writings had been used—and still were used by many churches and whole denominations—to keep women out of ministry and leadership. So this began to play on my mind.

THE BIBLE, WOMEN, AND THE CHURCH

I was sure that the Bible was not anti-women in general and not anti- the idea that women could do what they were called to do by God. I didn't read the Bible like that and although I could see that there was a male bias in general (it was written by men mostly about other men!), I thought that there was enough evidence in the Bible itself to give positive messages to women about their roles and potential in God's kingdom. I became more and more aware of the great gulf between my own understanding of Scripture, which had been shaped in a community that welcomed the ministry and leadership of women, and those who read Scripture as if it was saying the opposite. So I felt compelled to research. I started with 1 Corinthians 11 and I'm glad I did because it's been such an interesting journey.

I'm not really sure why I started there, but I soon discovered what a crucial text it has been and still is in relation to the place of women in church. I also discovered that although there are people who like to think that there is such a thing as a "plain-sense reading" of this text, that this couldn't be further from the truth.

This text has had a huge impact on Christian women through the ages. It has affected worship practices, church structures, church leadership, marriages, and even relationships between men and women in general. These fifteen verses play a central role in the thinking of many people. This is perplexing to say the least, because they are opaque—not transparent at all. In other words, not only is there not a "plain-sense reading" of these verses, but the more you study them, the more baffling they become.

SENSE AND NON-SENSE

That struck me as pretty serious. My thinking was this: if we are going to build whole systems of identity, relationship, and church practice on these verses, we should probably do our very best to understand what they mean! So I applied myself to the task. When I began to do this in earnest, I found an enormous level of confusion. I discovered confusion over the meaning of the words in the passage, confusion over Paul's intentions, and confusion as to how we should apply these verses today. In fact, that confusion is so severe that I was shocked by the idea that anyone at all could claim to be able to apply these verses in any straightforward manner whatsoever. And the truth is, they *never are* applied in a straightforward manner. Think for a minute how these verses have been and are being applied in churches throughout the world. Here are some examples of the confusion.

- Do women need to wear head coverings? Some say yes, and some say no.

- If yes, *what kind?* Hats, scarves, veils, handkerchiefs, anything we can find to hand?! (I heard of one woman who had a dirty dishcloth thrown on her head when she stood up to speak because it was the first cloth the woman next to her could find.)

- And *why* do women need to do this? They must do this as a sign of authority—but *whose* authority? Their own authority or someone else's authority? If someone else's, whose? God's, man's, their husband's?

- Should we forget the idea of a literal veil or head covering but still say that women need a (metaphorical) "covering"? Many churches apply this principle by ensuring that a man in authority is present when a woman speaks or ministers. Is this a correct interpretation of this passage?

- Or alternatively, is this about hairstyles? Do women only need to have long hair and not cut their hair?

- But should their hair be tied up?

- Do men need to have short hair? Nature, we are told, teaches you that if a man has long hair it's a disgrace. Is it?

- Is any of this relevant today?

- If so, do we teach this, practice it, or even *enforce* it?

- So finally, why have so many churches abandoned these practices all together?

You see what I mean. It's not clear at all. I discuss these issues in detail in *Women and Worship*. I'll summarize them in the course of this book.

AN INVESTIGATION . . .

I began to investigate; 1 Corinthians became my focus. What was Paul getting at? First, he tells men they *shouldn't* wear head coverings in church when they pray or prophesy. Then he tells women that they *should* wear head coverings when they are praying and prophesying. In one way that looks quite positive because at least he clearly thinks women should take part in the service by praying and prophesying—but why only if they covered their heads? This sounds strange. I knew that a lot of people assumed that his reasons must be cultural; women covered their heads at the time didn't they? So Christian women should cover their heads so as not to offend anyone. (Actually, you'll see that it's not as simple as that, but that's what many people assume is going on.) The real problem with all of that is that it's not the reason Paul gives.

PAUL'S REASONS

Here are the reasons that Paul gives:

The first reason he gives is that a man shouldn't cover his head because "man is the image and glory of God" (v. 7). So there's something in the way that man was created, how he is related to God, and how he is related to woman, which means that his head must be visible.

And what is the reason that women should cover their heads? Because a woman is the glory of man, not the image and glory of God (v. 7). There's something about the way she was created, how she is related to God, and how she is related to man, that means that her head must be invisible or covered. She comes from man (v. 8). She was created for man (v. 9). And because of the angels (v. 10)—whatever that means!

Those are not cultural reasons, but what is it all supposed to mean? Is it relevant to us today? If it is, should women still be covering their heads when they pray and prophesy? To add to the confusion, later on in the letter, he then tells the married women to keep quiet altogether! (1 Cor 14:33–36) All the rules and prohibitions seem odd, and even at odds with one another. They certainly don't fit with the picture we get of Paul and his female co-workers. Plus, the theology behind it all is peculiar. Studying this passage throws up multiple problems which we'll go on to discuss. I wanted to find some answers.

When I came across all the answers that have been given up until now, I have to tell you that they didn't convince me at all. Some of the answers were as muddled as the passage! I won't repeat all of that in this book. In this book, I want to take you on a journey of exploring this text to show you that it can't be read as straightforwardly as people think it can. And here's my issue. If it can't be read straightforwardly, then presumably, it can't be used in a straightforward manner to keep women out of ministry and leadership. If it's as muddled as you're going to see that it is, then it can't be used as "authoritative" in the debate about women because it's actually saying two things at once. Before I show you the confusion that this passage generates, I want you to do two things. First I want you to use the power of your imagination.

NEVER ASSUME . . .

In all of this, whatever we do or don't think, there is one thing that nearly all readers have in common. We assume that the problem was with the women. Most readers just assume that for some reason Paul must have needed to rebuke the women in Corinth. We're not entirely sure why they were doing what they were doing, but they were out of hand—behaving badly. It certainly could sound like that when you read it, and so that's generally where we start. Except that, when you read modern commentators on 1 Corinthians as a whole, they are nearly unanimous in claiming that Paul's main difficulty at Corinth was with the men! Paul was targeting the men. Paul was faced with domineering, gifted, factious (getting into warring groups), and arrogant men in the church in Corinth; men who were mostly concerned with their honor and status in the world's eyes.

So what happens if we make some different assumptions when we come to the text? What happens if we imagine a different scenario from the one we have previously assumed? What happens if, instead of some troublesome women at the heart of the church at Corinth, we envisage a group of domineering, gifted, and troublesome *men*?

THE POWER OF THE IMAGINATION

I began to imagine a different scenario. Paul had spent eighteen months in Corinth and then left. He left some people in charge but the people in the church began to fall out with each other. The leaders started behaving badly to the poor, and were arrogant and domineering. They were more concerned with how they looked to outsiders in terms of their honor and their status than how they were serving Christ. They were sexually immoral. Standards had totally slipped!

What if these men had taken charge in Paul's absence and decided that Paul had given the women way too much freedom when he was with them, and so after he left, they decided that the women needed to learn their place again, and conform to *their* rules? What if they felt threatened by the women playing some kind of equal role in worship? What if we imagine that this group of men had decided that women needed to wear head coverings when they were participating in the worship because, according to their own codes of shame and honor (not Paul's), they were shaming the men, Christ, God, and the angels if they refused to wear head coverings? Is this so far-fetched? It sounds so contemporary in a strange way—a scenario we're all used to. Men so easily behave like that toward women, and have done so throughout the whole of history.

What if Paul disagreed with them? What if 1 Corinthians 11:2–16 is his argument against them, telling them not to make women wear head coverings, but to leave them to pray and prophesy just as they are, because they have a head covering—their hair—and that is their glory?

I changed my mind and began to think differently. I began to think that Paul was correcting the men. But before I explain what I saw, I want you to do something else. I want you to think about the passage for yourself.

NO SUCH THING AS A STUPID QUESTION

I'd like you to read our passage through with a pen and paper next to you. As you're reading, imagine that Paul is sitting in front of you and that you have the chance to say anything you want to him or to ask him any question. Don't worry about offending him with your questions. He was used to debating so I feel sure he wouldn't mind! You have the chance to raise all the potential problems in the passage and to ask him anything you like. What will you say? Read the passage and make as many notes as you want for yourself, and then move on to chapter 1. I've taught on this passage for years now and I always ask people to be really honest about their responses. I find younger Christians find it easier than older ones, but that when people are honest about the difficulties that they have with the passage, it unlocks a catalog of questions and concerns with Paul's views expressed here. Pen and paper at the ready . . .

1 CORINTHIANS 11:2–16

2 I praise you for remembering me in everything and for holding to the traditions just as I passed them on to you. 3 But I want you to realize that the head of every man is Christ, and the head of the woman is man, and the head of Christ is God. 4 Every man who prays or prophesies with his head covered dishonors his head. 5 But every woman who prays or prophesies with her head uncovered dishonors her head—it is the same as having her head shaved. 6 For if a woman does not cover her head, she might as well have her hair cut off; but if it is a disgrace for a woman to have her hair cut off or her head shaved, then she should cover her head.

7 A man ought not to cover his head, since he is the image and glory of God; but woman is the glory of man. 8 For man did not come from woman, but woman from man; 9 neither was man created for woman, but woman

for man. 10 It is for this reason that a woman ought to have authority over her own head, because of the angels. 11 Nevertheless, in the Lord woman is not independent of man, nor is man independent of woman. 12 For as woman came from man, so also man is born of woman. But everything comes from God.

13 Judge for yourselves: Is it proper for a woman to pray to God with her head uncovered? 14 Does not the very nature of things teach you that if a man has long hair, it is a disgrace to him, 15 but that if a woman has long hair, it is her glory? For long hair is given to her as a covering. 16 If anyone wants to be contentious about this, we have no other practice—nor do the churches of God.

Do you have your questions and notes? Let's proceed.

1

1 Corinthians 11
Too Many Problems

I wonder what you wrote down. Here are some questions that might have come to mind.

1. What does it mean for a man to be the "head" of the woman if Christ is the "head" of man and God is the "head" of Christ?

2. Why does a man dishonor his head (Christ?) if he prays and prophesies with his head covered?

3. Why does a woman praying and prophesying with her head uncovered *dishonor* her head (and is her "head" a specific man or man in general?)? Why is this as bad as having your head shaved? What does that symbolize?

4. Does Paul think that a woman who disobeys him should have her head shaved? Does that sound threatening or harmless? Was he just exaggerating? How serious is the disgrace of not covering your head?

5. Paul gives theological reasons for men leaving their heads uncovered and women wearing head coverings. Man is the image and glory of God. Woman is the glory of man. Man does not come from woman. Man was not created for woman.

Woman comes from man and is created for him (vv. 7–9). This is the reason given for the need for head coverings, and because of the angels (v. 10). For this reason (these reasons), a woman ought to have a sign of authority on her head (a head covering?). Even though we may not understand the theology behind the ruling here the message is clear and unambiguous. Why do we not wear head coverings today? (Some people still think women should.)

6. Does Paul really believe that what we wear or how we have our hairstyles has *theological* significance in relation to gender roles and also to God? In other words, do we communicate something of the essence of being a man or a woman by our clothing, and does that also have spiritual significance? This passage answers "yes" to both those questions.

7. Why does Paul say "man" alone is the image and glory of God? If we compare this with Genesis 1:26–27, then we have two problems with this statement. One is that in Genesis 1, it is man and woman *together* who are the image of God and the other is that the writer of Genesis uses image and *likeness*, not image and glory. So this is not a direct quote from Genesis.

8. When you get to verse 11, however, it feels like Paul changes his mind. Now he says that "in the Lord" woman is not independent of man, and man is not independent of woman. Having said first that man didn't come from woman, he now says that he does! So we are interdependent after all, and we all come from each other. So what has happened to the reason for the head coverings? Is that now redundant?

9. Look again at verse 14. Does Paul really think that the "nature of things" teaches us how we should wear our hair and what length it should be? What does he mean by that? Isn't it God who teaches us how things should be, or does "nature" have a special place in Paul's thought so that "nature" is a synonym for God? If that's the case, does this mean that Christian boys and men should never have long hair?

10. Is he saying in the end that a woman's *hair* is her glory (v. 15)? Does this mean she can have long hair *instead of* a head covering?

11. What is the practice that he says they don't have in any other church? "We have no such custom!" (v. 16) He clearly strongly disapproves of anyone who disagrees with him on this. If that's the practice of women going bare-headed, then we have to ask again, why don't we wear head coverings today? Surely, it's still a disgrace. But strangely, if he does mean that he has no such custom of women going bare-headed in any of his churches, why don't we hear about it in any of his other letters?

12. Finally, why does it seem like there are contradictions or at least real inconsistencies between verses 2–10 and verses 11–16?

Those questions and problems should all come about just by reading the text without any need for any knowledge of the scholarship. I hope you got some of them if not all of them. Maybe you had even more! What if we look at the scholarship on the passage? Unfortunately, not only does this not solve our problems, this only throws up further confusion.

THE SCHOLARS' PROBLEMS

Here are some of the knottier problems that are present in the text once you know what's going on with the language, and this will give you some idea of how this passage can be read completely differently by different people, even when they know a lot!

LOST IN TRANSLATION

One of the main difficulties for a scholar is how we translate the words and phrases that we find here. Don't forget that you are reading a translation of the original language—Greek. The Greek used in the Bible is called "Koine Greek" (pronounced koy-nay) and means the "common Greek" from the time when the Bible was written. Just like with English, there are different dialects of Greek, so Bible scholars need to know Koine Greek to understand what words and phrases would have meant to the readers at the time. Sometimes it's easy to work out what a word meant. Say you have a common word, like "sheep" or "jar" or "wine," and it always means the same thing wherever it appears both in the Bible and in other texts written at the same time, then it will be easy to translate it when it appears. Suppose, however, that you have a word that appears nowhere else (or hardly anywhere else) outside your passage, then that is going to make the job of translation harder. Scholars have to look carefully at the word in its context, then whether it appears somewhere else in the Bible, then in other texts, and then make their best well-educated guess as to its meaning. They might be spot on, but then again, they might not be 100 percent accurate. Sometimes discoveries of other texts as the centuries go by mean that scholars change their minds or revise older texts.

In our passage, there is uncertainty about how to understand the precise meaning of *all* the crucial terms and phrases in this passage. These terms include: "head," "uncovered," "glory," "authority over her head," "because of the angels," "in the place of a shawl," "such a custom," and "man" and "woman," which could equally mean "husband" and "wife." We'll look at these in more detail as we go on. This means that scholars debate and disagree over the meaning of *all* these words. If you check these against the passage, you'll see that this means the entire meaning of the passage is under discussion. Imagine then what a difference it will make to the translation depending on how you choose to translate any particular word. I will show you some of the choices that we have as we go through the book.

HEAD COVERINGS OR HAIRSTYLES?

First, and importantly, scholars are divided about whether Paul is talking about "head covering" or "hair length" and "hairstyles."

This is because the Greek expression in verse 4 can either mean "having down *on* the head" or "having down *from* the head." It can be translated either way. If we follow the first translation—*on* the head—we would take it to mean a head covering. If we follow the second one—*from* the head—we would take it to mean long hair. The argument for hairstyles rather than head coverings is also supported by the references to hair length in verses 14–15. There is a total lack of agreement as to which is meant precisely in verse 4, but the weight of scholarship, simply in terms of the number of serious Corinthian scholars who opt for one or the other, is with head coverings. In other words, the hairstyles reading is currently a minority view. That in itself doesn't mean that the minority is wrong, but in this case I think verse 4 is referring to head coverings, even though later verses refer to hair length. I'll explain why below.

WHY SUCH A SHAME?

Some scholars like to say that Paul must have wanted women to wear head coverings (or have their hair a certain way) because of the "culture." The thinking is that what must have been uppermost in Paul's mind is that he wanted to win people for Christ, and he wouldn't have wanted to put a stumbling block in anyone's way. If all women in your culture wore head coverings because it was shameful to do otherwise, then it wouldn't be a good idea if the church bucked the trend. If outsiders walked in, they would be shocked to see women bare-headed; it would only alienate them and defeat the task of mission. It's not a bad idea to be sensitive to those around you if you are trying to convince people about the truth of the gospel. Paul even says earlier in the letter that he became like a Jew to win the Jews, like one under the law to win those under the law, like one outside the law to win those outside the law etc. (1 Cor 9:19–23). But is that what he was doing here? I don't think so.

First of all, nobody is quite sure which customs from which group Paul might have been referring to when he said that head coverings shame a man, and a bare head shames a woman. The Corinthian church was made up of Jews, Romans, and Greeks. They all had different customs when it came to head coverings and hairstyles and these customs were different again depending on whether they were out on the streets, at home, or in worship. For example, Jewish men would be used to having their heads covered, especially at prayer, and wealthy Roman women would have been used not to having their heads covered. It's very difficult to declare with confidence what exactly *was* shameful or honoring in terms of what people wore—and especially what they wore in worship—particularly as there were different rules within different sections of society. So it raises the questions: Which group would Paul have been trying to please? How? And why? His "rules" were not universally applicable.

Others say that Paul was concerned that men looked like real men and women looked like real women. So this is about the difference between the sexes that is reflected in what we wear. Paul was concerned that the men weren't effeminate and that the women weren't butch, and that Christians shouldn't do the equivalent of "cross-dressing." There are also some scholars who think that the shame was about the men appearing gay and the women appearing to be lesbian. I don't think there's much evidence for either of these views. This is just reading something into the text that it doesn't say and ignoring what it does say.

Remember that the passage gives a very explicit reason for the shame. The shame is not caused by the society around you, but the fact that you will shame the one who is your "head" and, of course, because of the angels. This is not a cultural reason in the passage. This is a reason that is supposedly rooted in the creation order of women, men, Christ, God, and the angels. It refers to how the cosmos was ordered. This passage makes a clear link between the shame, the physical head and what you wear on your physical head, and the metaphysical spiritual head. In other words, what happens in reality and real relations of men and women in church is linked to an abstract or symbolic spiritual reality of the relationship of women, men, God, and angels. We're actually not really able to establish precisely what that link might be, but we'll come back to that. For now, we simply ask what is the reason for the shame?

The most obvious reading of these verses is that men should not be shamed by covering up their glory (which is theirs because they are the image of God/Christ) and that women, who have no glory of their own, should not shame men by being uncovered. Being uncovered is probably a sign that they are either acting above their station, or behaving like men, or rejecting an outward sign of authority. There's a fundamental inequality between the two "sources" of shame. Paul says on the one hand that men should not cover their heads (their own glory) because they are the glory of God, but that women, who are also men's glory, should be covered. Why should one source of glory be covered and the other uncovered?

It's difficult to avoid the message that according to this passage, women have no "glory" of their own, and no *direct* relation to the image of God; their image and glory is *via* the man. The bottom line is that the women lack something that the men have and the covering makes up for it. We'll look at this in more detail in chapter 3. Let's carry on with the difficulties that we face with this passage.

WHAT WE DON'T KNOW

There is a lot then, that we don't know. This doesn't mean that we can't piece things together, but we need to realize that that is what we are doing: piecing something together from bits of information and then filling in the gaps. If we knew more, for instance, about the precise situation in Corinth, or why Paul was worried about the angels, or what custom he was referring to that he doesn't have in any other of his churches, this would help, but we don't.

We don't actually know that much about practices in the early church because we have very little written evidence of what exactly early Christians did when they got together, and how they did it. We know they ate together and celebrated the Lord's Supper. They had baptisms, sang hymns, listened to Scripture being recited, and prayed and prophesied. We know they met in homes. We know that whole households were present, the master, the mistress, the children, the slaves, the slaves' children, but we don't know exactly what that looked like. We construct scenarios to make sense of the text. But this means that our historical reconstructions of the situations in the early church and here in Corinth are highly speculative. They have a lot of guesswork in them. This is true of my own reconstruction as well. Readers need to know this when they're being offered explanations of this passage, and try to be discerning about what they read. How do we do this?

HOW DO WE MAKE DECISIONS?

Some people get nervous about the idea that we "question" the Bible, but asking questions of difficult texts in the Bible doesn't mean either that we are doubting the authority of Scripture or that we are casting doubt on the coherence of the message. Some passages really are quite straightforward and easy to understand, but this is not true of the whole Bible. When we come to passages and stories that we don't immediately understand, wrestling with the text is an act of faith. It's saying that we do believe there is something of worth to find. On top of this, we need to know what to do when we discover that Bible-believing, Spirit-filled, God-loving Christians can read the same texts and come up with radically different answers. Where do we turn and what do we do when we discover there's a conflict?

When faced with conflicting opinions about what the Bible "says," you will need to weigh up what you are hearing against what you know to be true of God from your own reading of Scripture and what your own community/denomination holds to be true. The weight of church tradition and the majority consensus is important, but as individuals, if we find that the church has always thought a certain way on an issue, we need to know why, and to weigh that up as well. All Christians, as far as is possible, should make informed decisions.

This will mean listening to your community and tradition, reading about all sides of an argument, and making a decision based on what you believe to be the best argument with the strongest case, in conjunction with your own Spirit-led intuition. At the end of the day, we should aim to read the Bible with integrity. This means making informed and intelligent decisions that we can believe in and most importantly, live by.

I hope that I have demonstrated to you that this is the situation we find ourselves in with 1 Corinthians 11:2–16. We don't have easy answers on a plate and we have quite a task ahead of us trying to make sense of this passage, but it doesn't mean that we shouldn't try. The passage itself invites us to dig deep.

THE PROBLEM WITH THE WOMEN

I mentioned in the introduction that everyone assumes that Paul had trouble with the women. This seems reasonable enough on the surface, but I want to paint a picture for you about the nature and the extent of the problem if this were to be the case—I mean if it really was the women who were the problem—just so you're sure about what might really have been going on.

The church at Corinth, like all of Paul's churches, would have had Christian women converts, many of whom would have been slaves. Although it was possible for some wealthy women to have had quite a few freedoms in the society of the time, most of these women would have felt the effects of being brought up in an overtly patriarchal society—a society where men held most of the positions of power and influence. For most women, this would have meant that they were second-class citizens in terms of their status and their rights. They were born inferior, and they knew it. Slaves were the property of their masters and could be used for sex at a master's whim (this was true of female and male slaves). Wealthy women were better off than slave women, and married women who ran households had considerable authority and responsibilities in their own spheres. But all married women were the property either of their husbands or sometimes still their fathers depending on the conditions of their marriage. Unmarried girls were the property of their menfolk. There were also educated women who had some degree of empowerment and autonomy in the public sphere, and some of them were backed and supported by men, but these were exceptions rather than the rule.

What happened when women in this cultural context became Christians? We know for sure that Paul allowed women to pray and prophesy at Corinth. We also know that Christian slaves and masters and men and women now ate together in a church setting, and that the Christian table was not one where the wealthy and powerful had priority. So although in the society of the time becoming a Christian didn't lead directly to a change in status, when they were worshipping together in church, their social status was overridden by their status "in Christ." The oppressive practices of their society were supposed to be overturned in the way they related to one another as believers. No one was better or worse, superior or inferior. They were all one. You could say that the church was supposed to be little taste of heaven.

PAUL'S WOMEN

From the rest of Paul's writings we know that Paul worked very closely with many women. In Romans he names Mary, Tryphaena, Tryphosa, and Persis as friends and co-laborers (Rom 16:6, 12). He also describes Euodia and Syntyche as those who labored side by side with him (Phil 4:3). He was happy with women as leaders of house churches (Lydia in Acts 16:14–15, Phoebe in Rom 16:1, and Nympha in Col 4:15). Priscilla and her husband, Aquila, were both church leaders and Paul's co-workers. Where Priscilla is mentioned first (Acts 18:18, 26; Rom 16:3; 2 Tim 4:19), it signifies that she has some kind of priority in the relationship and in Paul's mind. Paul stayed with them in Corinth so they must have been great friends of his and they both discipled Apollos in the faith (Acts 18:26). This challenges the idea that Paul prevented women from teaching men.

A further challenge to this idea comes through what we know of Phoebe and Junia. Phoebe not only led a church at Cenchreae, but was also the person who delivered the letter to the Roman church and would have read it aloud to them. As this would have required also memorizing and interpreting the letter, this elevates Phoebe to the status of a teacher with profound theological insight. Finally, we now know that Paul even refers to his friend and co-worker Junia as an apostle (Rom 16:7).

We know from our own passage here that he is clearly happy with women prophesying and praying in public (even if we don't understand the head coverings), and we know that he obviously approves of Philip's four daughters who were known as prophets (Acts 21:9). Interestingly, in 1 Corinthians, Paul describes the gift of prophecy as being that which builds up the *whole* church, so prophets would have spoken to the whole church and had considerable authority in the gathering. Not only this, but in 1 Corinthians 12:28 he talks about there being *first* apostles, *second* prophets, and *third* teachers. The order that he places them in here is not an accident and shows us that he put prophecy before teaching in terms of importance. Paul recognized women as apostles, prophets, and teachers. He wasn't anti-women in leadership, and he didn't shut them down. He recognized their gifts and worked side by side with them in mission. So what would have been happening at Corinth for the women to be troublesome enough for Paul to intervene and to get them back into order?

WOMEN OUT OF CONTROL

What certain scholars propose is that in this newfound liberated existence, initially encouraged by Paul, women in Corinth have now developed ideas above their station, and are behaving inappropriately. Given an inch, they have taken a mile, and have started throwing off the head coverings as a sign of their new liberation. But Paul didn't mean them to go that far! This is serious because throwing off a head covering is a shameful and even disgusting practice.

Other scholars develop this idea, imagining that the women were not just taking off their head coverings in quiet protest (which might have been an option), but whipping themselves up into a charismatic frenzy, refusing to be told what to do, and behaving in a way that would have reminded people of the temple prostitutes of their time, or loose adulterous women. In other words, they were wanton. Whatever the reason, and whatever it looked like, the idea is that the women had thrown all caution to the wind, and were behaving with the utmost disrespect in church, not caring who they shamed: themselves, their fathers, husbands, sons, uncles, God, Christ, and the angels. They didn't care what they looked like to the outside world. They didn't even care whether they were being seen to be behaving like prostitutes and adulterers in a worship service.

If this is true, then how were the men responding? It's important to spell this out as well, and there are three possible options.

1. The men might have been colluding and joining in with their own version of bad behavior (i.e., covering their heads or growing their hair long). This means that it could have become a problem that had "infected" the entire church.

2. The women's menfolk were overlooking the offense, not realizing the seriousness of what was happening, and so Paul needed to intervene to get everyone in order.

3. Perhaps the men had tried to correct their womenfolk but the women wouldn't listen. This means that they weren't listening to their fathers, their husbands, their church leaders, (possibly even some fellow women), who had presumably pleaded with them not to behave so badly in public.

Any one of these, or a mixture of all three, needed to be happening in order to require the intervention of the apostle himself on this issue. We are required to imagine here that what they were doing was so bad and so serious that Paul insisted on intervening.

THE SERIOUSNESS OF THE CRIME

The seriousness of the behavior is spelled out in verse 6, and here I'll give you a number of different translations so you can see how scholars have tried to interpret what Paul might have meant. Supposedly, Paul goes on to say either,

> For if a woman will not veil herself, then she should cut off her hair; but if it is disgraceful for a woman to have her hair cut off or to be shaved, she should wear a veil. (NRSV)

or,

> For if a woman does not cover her head, she might as well have her hair cut off; but if it is a disgrace for a woman to have her hair cut off or her head shaved, then she should cover her head. (NIV)

or,

> For if a woman does not cover her head, let her also have her hair cut off; but if it is disgraceful for a woman to have her hair cut off or her head shaved, let her cover her head. (NAS)

or,

> For if the woman be not covered, let her also be shorn: but if it be a shame for a woman to be shorn or shaven, let her be covered. (KJV)

You can see that some translations soften the reading as if to say, if a woman is so willful that she wishes to go unveiled, she should be willing to go the whole hog and just cut her hair off! In other words, she may as well cut her (own) hair. This clearly takes the edge off any implication that "she should be shorn" by someone else, which sounds horrible. You could paraphrase an inoffensive interpretation of this verse like this:

> *If a woman is intent on shaming her "head"* (her own head and man/her husband) *by throwing off her head covering or letting down her hair, she may as well go the whole way*

and just cut off her hair, but if/as that is equally shameful, she should remain covered.

That makes it sound more like a warning or advice. But what if Paul was saying something like, "a woman should be shorn"? That is more like an aggressive punishment. In order to get away from how bad that sounds, some scholars say that Paul must have been exaggerating to make a point. It's a figure of speech called hyperbole (pronounced hy-*per*-bolee) that tells us we shouldn't take it literally. But some interpretations do make it sound like a real threat, so that we get the impression that it sounds like this:

> *If a woman does not cover her head, she should have her head shaved. She is flagrantly disgracing herself and man/ the men/her husband, and so should be made an example of with a sign of public disgrace. But as this is equally shameful, she should be covered.*

Women *were* sometimes forced to shave their heads or have their heads shaved as a sign of public shaming and this practice endured for centuries. In France, after the Second World War, the women who had had sexual relations with Nazis (often against their will and/or in order to feed their children) were treated as traitors and Nazi collaborators. Their punishment was to have their heads shaved, to be branded with a swastika, and to be paraded barefoot through the streets. It was the deepest form of humiliation. The fact that the passage equates taking off a head covering with such a severe punishment tells us a bit about the importance of the head covering. We shouldn't gloss over this message. Bruce Winter writes the following on the significance of the shorn woman:

> Paul made a startling statement about the unveiled wife. He said that her behaviour was "one and the same thing as a woman who has been shorn" (11.5). It is known, e.g., that in Cyprus the law prescribed that "a woman guilty of adultery shall have her hair cut off and be a prostitute," i.e., like a foreigner or freedwoman who provided sexual favours at a dinner. Therefore, *Paul equated not wearing a veil with the social stigma of a publicly exposed and*

punished adulteress reduced to the status of a prostitute.[1]
[emphasis added]

So whether this is an intended punishment or not, even if it's a form of hyperbole, what we can take away from the reference is that going without a head covering is a serious crime.

Winter makes another point on the seriousness of the crime referred to here. Paul uses the term "ought" twice in these verses, in verse 7 and verse 10. A man "ought" not to cover his head, and a woman "ought" to have a sign of authority on her head. Winter says that the use of this word shows us that Paul is using "the most powerful argument that could be used in correcting conduct in the first century."[2] In other words, Paul is saying, "You *must* do this!" It is not a take-it-or-leave-it suggestion; it's a strong rebuke about a very serious and shameful practice.

Regardless of what the women and the men were doing wrong, whether this is concerning head coverings or hairstyles, Paul is saying that the behavior of the women is equivalent to the behavior of whores and adulterers, so they may as well be treated as such. Even if you wanted to say that Paul was using forceful language simply to enforce his point, it's pretty shocking. Remember as well that the men have no punishment or threat hanging over them for the misdemeanor of covering their heads.

SETTING THE SCENE

So we're asked to imagine all kinds of scenarios in order to make sense of Paul's thought, and they're all based on the assumption that it's the *women* who are rebellious and non-compliant. I am not for one second implying that women can never be rebellious, wild, and non-compliant. I am simply testing the hypothesis by spelling out the full extent of what we are required to believe if we accept this reading. I'm also questioning whether it really is easier to imagine a group of Christian women in a patriarchal society

1. Winter, *After Paul,* 128.
2. Ibid., 130–31.

to have become so wild and rebellious, and so disrespectful and uncontrollable in opposition to their menfolk, that they need the intervention of the apostle, or whether maybe it's easier to imagine the opposite? I personally find it easier to imagine the existence of a group of spiritually gifted and highly articulate male teachers who were both overbearing and divisive, and who believed that women should be kept in their place.

If we do think that the problem was with the men, and not with the women, it means that we have to read the passage completely differently. As we shall see, it means that Paul was *opposing* the practice of head coverings for women, not enforcing it; he was *liberating* women, not oppressing them, and he was coming against those who were. In the next chapter, I'll explain how I see this working.

2

Paul in Conversation

We've started to raise some of the many difficulties with our passage and now I want to show you how we might be able to resolve some of them. In order to do this, I need to give you some background on the letter of 1 Corinthians and what we know of Paul's writing style. We know that Paul left Corinth and went to Ephesus. When he was there he received reports of what was happening in Corinth as well as having some correspondence with the church. Paul had already written once to the Corinthians and they had written back (1 Cor 5:9). Our letter is his reply to their reply. What we know as *1* Corinthians is actually the *second* letter he wrote to them, so reading our 1 Corinthians is like reading a string of emails in which only one person's emails remain while the other person's responses have been deleted.[1]

We can see evidence in 1 Corinthians that Paul is referring to subjects that the Corinthians had already written to him about and he's replying to them on certain issues. When you read 1 Corinthians, you'll see that editors have decided that there are times when Paul quotes a Corinthian phrase or idea (often called a slogan). There are no quotation marks in the Greek to tell us when he might be doing this, but the sense of the letter tells us that it's likely

1. I'm grateful to Scot McKnight for this comparison.

he's doing it in 6:12–13; 7:1; 8:1, 4; and 10:23. That's why editors have inserted quotation marks into the text, to help us make better sense of it. Thus, editors assume that when Paul wrote, "Everything is permissible for me" (6:12), he is, in fact, quoting a Corinthian phrase that he's about to disagree with or modify. The Corinthians say, "Everything is permissible for me," and Paul replies, "but not everything is beneficial." The Corinthians say, "Everything is permissible for me," and Paul replies, "I will not be mastered by anything."

But let me show you two interesting examples of where editors haven't yet made up their minds about what might be Paul's voice and what might be the Corinthians' voices, and how that changes the meaning of the passage. There are two verses in 1 Corinthians where scholars are divided over where the quotation actually ends. One is 6:13 and the other is 8:8. Here are the choices.

1 Corinthians 6:13 could be divided up like this:
Choice Number One

> **Corinthians:** Food for the stomach and the stomach for food
>
> **Paul:** but God will destroy them both
>
> **Paul:** The body is not meant for sexual immorality, but for the Lord, and the Lord for the body.

Or like this:
Choice Number Two

> **Corinthians:** Food for the stomach and the stomach for food, but God will destroy them both.
>
> **Paul:** The body is not meant for sexual immorality, but for the Lord, and the Lord for the body.

Richard Hays (a New Testament scholar) has the second version in his book, *The Moral Vision of the New Testament*, so he's gone ahead and made a decision that the whole sentence reflects Corinthian thought.[2] Why would he do that?

---

2. Hays, *The Moral Vision*, loc. 1420.

Is it Paul or the Corinthians who are saying that God will destroy both food and the stomach? The Corinthians, apparently, had an idea that following Jesus meant that they could still do whatever they wanted with their bodies and in their sex lives because "everything is permissible." They also had a strong body/spirit divide where they had convinced themselves that what they did in the body didn't affect their "spiritual" life, so they were arguing with Paul that it doesn't matter what we do in the body because the spirit is free from that. This was their excuse for having sex with prostitutes! If the stomach is made for food and the body is made for sex, you may as well indulge. If you add the second half of the sentence to the Corinthian slogan, what they're saying is, you may as well indulge because God is going to destroy the material world anyway.

This last idea makes more sense in the mouth of the Corinthians than in the mouth of Paul who is trying to persuade them that their bodies are temples of the Holy Spirit and should be treated as holy vessels for the Lord. According to Paul, it really *does* matter what we do in our bodies, because our bodies are the seeds of our eternal beings. God is not going to destroy our bodies, he's going to resurrect them! He's going to resurrect the very same bodies we have lived in all our lives. Paul explains all of this in detail in 1 Corinthians 15. I think in years to come we'll find that the whole of the sentence is in quotation marks in many Bibles.

The second example is in 8:8 and is linked to the ideas that we've just looked at in 6:13—the question of the importance of the body, how we use it, and what we put into it. It reads like this, "But food does not bring us near to God; we are no worse if we do not eat, and no better if we do." In the NIV or the ESV you won't find any quotation marks in 8:8. If you look at the NRSV, however, you'll see that the editors have made a decision to put the first half of the verse in quotes, "Food will not bring us close to God." Now if you look at the footnote to that verse you will see this "The quotation may extend to the end of the verse." The same suggestion that we found in 6:13! What difference does it make to our interpretation if half or even the whole of 8:8 is Corinthian thought?

If the whole of 8:8 is Corinthian, then this follows on the theme of Paul referring to their overdeveloped sense of their own freedom; that they can just do what they want. He responds to them in 8:9 "Be careful, however, that the exercise of your freedom does not become a stumbling-block to the weak," or in the NRSV it reads, "But take care that this liberty of yours does not somehow become a stumbling block to the weak." In the Greek, Paul uses "but" in 8:9 implying that he is disagreeing with or modifying something that they've said.

So you see, Paul is in conversation and we're still not entirely sure where the lines are between his thought and the Corinthians. We know that he's trying to correct them on certain issues and to persuade them of his own views. We also know that it's as if he's showing them that they're wrong by using the type of argument that goes: "you say this . . . , but I say this . . . ." The problem is that he doesn't necessarily always say "you say" and "I say" first. It's not such an unusual idea that he should do this. First of all, we know that this was a common way of arguing at the time (sometimes called diatribal or rhetorical argumentation), and we also know that Paul used this technique in 1 Corinthians in various places. I'm suggesting that he does this *more* than was previously thought. Let's now turn to 1 Corinthians 11.

PLAUSIBLE . . . ?

We've seen then that Paul might be citing the Corinthians more than we thought. And the idea that Paul is citing the Corinthians in larger sections is something that a number of scholars have proposed.[3] As early as 1923, a biblical scholar and medical

---

3. There are a few contemporary scholars who see one form of rhetorical argument or another in 1 Corinthians 11:2–16. I think my work is the most developed so far, but I'm not the only one arguing that this might be the case in principle. For other examples, see Gilbert Bilezikian, Alan Padgett, Thomas Shoemaker, and Jose Vadakkedom. I discovered these as I began to research it as an idea. There are now numerous scholars who argue that 1 Corinthians 14:33b–35 represents Corinthian thought that Paul is responding to and refuting.

missionary called Katharine Bushnell put forward the proposal that 1 Corinthians 14:33b–35 is a quotation articulating the ideas of Paul's opponents' at Corinth. I discovered her work after I had written *Women and Worship* because someone read my book and sent me Bushnell's book saying that he thought I'd be interested in her work.

She argues this:

> To repeat: We are driven to believe *the Apostle was not ut-tering his own views* in verses 34 and 35 of 1 Cor. ch. 14, which read: *"Let the women keep silence in the churches: for it is not permitted unto them to speak: but let them be in subjection, as also saith the law. And if they would learn anything, let them ask their husbands at home: for it is a shame for women to speak in the church"* (R.V.) We believe this is the language of Judaizers at Corinth, which has been reported to Paul, and which Paul quotes to an-swer back in the words: *"What! came the word of God out from you? or came it unto you only?"*—with what follows to the end of the chapter.[4]

Not surprisingly, she anticipates people criticizing her argument and writes this:

> We merely wish to show that this idea that Paul makes quotations from the letter he has received and is answer-ing, is no novel idea, invented by us to suit the prejudiced view. Prof. Sir William Ramsay says, on this subject: *"We should be ready to suspect Paul is making a quotation from the letter addressed to him by the Corinthians whenever he alludes to their knowledge, or when any statement stands in marked contrast either with the immediate context or with Paul's known views."*[5]

Professor Sir William Ramsay was a contemporary of Bushnell's. He was a respected scholar of classical archaeology, an expert in Asia Minor, and a researcher of Paul and his journeys. What I find

---

4. Bushnell, *God's Word*, para. 203.

5. Ibid., para 205.

interesting here is Ramsay's criteria for assigning a particular view to Paul's opponents:

> . . . or when any statement stands in marked contrast either with the immediate context or with Paul's own views.

Bushnell applies his criteria to 1 Corinthians 14:33–36, as I also did nearly a hundred years later. It is also a reasonably simple step to go on and apply this criteria to 1 Corinthians 11:2–16.

CUES AND CLUES

What other clues do we have that Paul might be referring to a Corinthian idea? I see the same pattern in three places: 1 Corinthians 11:2–16; 14:20–25; and 14:33–36. These patterns function as clues that Paul is referring to ideas that are not his own. One of the most significant clues that we have in these passages is their ability to confuse the reader. We've looked at that with Paul's change of views starting at verse 11. Paul is often described as being "double-minded" in 1 Corinthians 11:2–16. But what if an explanation for Paul's double-mindedness is that there are actually two "minds" at work and two voices present in the text? Paul and the Corinthians are in the middle of a dialogue. Is this what we are listening to? In Ramsay's words, we're faced with a situation with statements that stand "in marked contrast either with the immediate context or with Paul's known views." So my conclusion was that it is precisely those things which we find confusing and baffling about the texts that are the clue to understanding them.

HOW THE CONVERSATION GOES

Below is the explanation of how I think we can divide up the text into Paul's voice and the Corinthian voice. The Corinthian voice is in italics and the rest is Paul. I have added some punctuation in the first section to give an indication of Paul's expression or "tone of voice," and have combined different translations, rather than relying solely on one version of Scripture. I'll add some commentary here, but this is to give you a picture of how I think the passage can be read, and then in the final two chapters of the book, I'll demonstrate in more detail why I have attributed certain ideas to the Corinthians instead of Paul. Finally, I want to show you that if we want to continue to claim that all these ideas belong to Paul, we're faced with some deep challenges in integrating his thought, his theology, and his practices, and in building a coherent and Christ-centered theology out of his writings.

BLENDED IDEAS

Because I couldn't reconcile Paul's ideas in 1 Corinthians 11, first within the text itself and then to his wider thought, I began to explore the possibilities that he was representing other people's ideas. The idea that a church would adopt a teacher's ideas and then corrupt them down the line, especially in a teacher's absence, is pretty much a normal course of events. It's the root of most Christian heresies.

Paul spent an initial eighteen months in Corinth evangelizing, teaching, and discipling. He was their pastor and they would have received all their teaching from him. When he left, however, they were left to their own devices, and it would have been a very natural process for them to have modified Paul's teaching in different ways, especially where it clashed with their own deeply embedded cultural assumptions. Like all Christians, the Corinthians would have continued to have been influenced by their surrounding culture and things that they already knew to be true before they had become Christians.

We know that this is happening in Corinth with their obsession with shame and honor, their desire for worldly status, their laissez-faire attitude to food sacrificed to idols, and their sexual immorality. They also had some strange ideas about their identity in Christ. They thought they were super-spiritual, they didn't understand about the resurrection, and they were in some confusion about the Trinity. This wasn't what Paul had taught them or what he wanted for them. They had allowed the "world" and their own philosophies to dominate their thinking and practices rather than being centered on Christ and the cross.

Paul adamantly disagrees with the Corinthians on certain ideas and practices. However, it's most likely that Paul is actually confronting a blend of his own teaching (albeit somewhat corrupted), ideas from the surrounding culture, and the thinking of this early Christian community itself. If you've ever tried to work out exactly what you agree with and disagree with in the teaching of a particular church or movement, you'll know that it's not a very straightforward process. It's a bit like trying to unpick a very tangled knot. This is what we're trying to do when we read 1 Corinthians.

I'm suggesting that the Corinthians have taken some Christian teaching, some ideas from Scripture, and even some of Paul's teaching, and blended it with their own ideas (cultural and religious) to come up with teachings and practices that were oppressive to women, all in the name of doing what they thought was "honorable" in the sight of God and to avoid shame.

1 CORINTHIANS 11:2–16 AS A RHETORICAL TEXT

My proposal rests on the idea that the Corinthians constructed a "theology" of head coverings based on Paul's teaching on the "head" and the relationship of God to Christ, Christ to man, and man to woman, and then added a number of other ideas to that. For this reason, Paul praises them for the traditions and teachings that they've held on to since he left. In other words, they're not *all* wrong. However, they misunderstood the teaching on headship to imply that men have a privileged and more glorious role above women because they have a mistaken view that man alone is the image and glory of God and woman derives her glory from her relationship with man. This is in the first half of our passage. In the second half of our passage, and in the letter overall, Paul corrects them, reminding them that in the end God is head over everything, which means that all things come from him, are under him, and will return to him. He puts this idea to them in verse 12, reminding them that everything comes from God, and in chapter 15, he comes back to this theme, where he reminds them that God will be "all in all" (1 Cor 15:28).

Here is how I see the passage being interpreted with a rhetorical reading.

THE TEXT

Paul writes:

> I praise you for remembering me in everything and for holding to the traditions/teachings, just as I passed them on to you. But I want you to have understood that the head of every man is Christ, and the head of the woman is man, but the head of Christ is God.

Paul has praised them for paying attention to some of his teaching. The Corinthians, however, have taken the theology of "headship" to an extreme to argue that women should have a covering over their physical heads to demonstrate that they are "covered" by their spiritual heads (men). This is the only way that they and the spiritual heads (men, Christ, God, even angels) will not be shamed. The Corinthians have given their rationale for this to Paul in a previous letter, and here we have it in front of us in 1 Corinthians. The Corinthian men have told the women that having their heads uncovered is so shameful that it's as bad as being in public with a shaved head—it's equivalent to the shame of a prostitute or adulteress. So we could insert a "You say . . ." here.

> *Every man who prays or prophesies with his head covered dishonors his head. And every woman who prays or prophesies with her head uncovered dishonors her head—it is just as though her head were shaved.*

We could read this two ways. Either they may even have threatened to cut off the hair of the women who were refusing to do what they told them to do. Or Paul may have been pushing them on the extreme nature of their theology of head coverings for women. Are you *really* saying that if a woman refuses to wear a head covering when she prays in public that she is behaving like an adulterer and a prostitute? I think this is more likely. If so, he responds by taking their reasoning to its logical absurd conclusion. In other words, he demonstrates with a question how the Corinthians have trapped the women into head coverings:

> So if a woman does not cover her head, she should have her hair cut off; and if it is a disgrace for a woman to have her hair cut or shaved off, she should cover her head!?

He then goes on to cite their reasons for this practice, which he's going to refute in the next section, but here he spells it out. We could insert another "You say . . ." here.

> *A man ought not to cover his head, since he is the image and glory of God; but the woman is the glory of man. For man did not come from woman, but woman from man; neither was man created for woman, but woman for man. For this reason, and because of the angels, the woman ought to have a sign of authority on her head.*

In the next chapter I'll explain how deeply problematic these ideas are if they are Paul's. For now, I want you to notice the reasons given here for *why* it's shameful for a woman to be without a head covering. The reason is because she has no glory of her own, but she is the glory of man. In other words, she has a derived glory from the male. Her glory is *in him.* She comes from him (i.e., was created from him), but more than that, she was created *for* him. Her whole identity is formed only in relation to the male and so her relationship with God is mediated through the man—he stands between her and God. It is for "this reason" and "because of the angels" that she *absolutely must* have a sign of authority on her head. This is not a cultural reason, but a reason rooted in creation (how things were from the beginning) and cosmology (how the universe is now constructed—the angels are included as well). We can't accept an interpretation of these verses that ignores the *theological* reasons given for head coverings and tries to persuade us that it's only cultural. It's not.

A CHANGE OF TACK

Then we come to verse 11. Verse 11 is important because there is a word here that signals a break in thought in the Greek, as if there is going to be a change of tack. The word is *plen* and doesn't come out very well in the English, especially as we often translate the Greek word as "nevertheless." This loses some of its impact. It's better translated, "The *point* is . . ." or "But what I'm saying is . . . ."

So first of all, it seems as if Paul is changing the thought process here, but also, in terms of the content of the passage, he is certainly going back on what he supposedly has just said! In my reading though, rather than thinking that Paul says one thing and then back-tracks on what he just said, we now go back to Paul's voice and his own thoughts on men and women, which are opposed to the Corinthians' views just set out. It could begin something like, "Actually, the point is . . ."

> . . . in the Lord, woman is not independent of/separated from man, nor is man independent of/separated from woman. For as woman came from man, so also man is born of woman. But everything comes from God.

According to Paul, men and women have a new status now "in the Lord," which means that they are not independent, but interdependent. However, it is not just their new status "in the Lord" that is significant for Paul as he sees their mutuality and interdependence rooted way back in creation.

The creation story in Genesis 2 that tells us that woman "comes from" man, but Paul doesn't read this as saying that this means that woman is totally dependent on man, was created *for* him, and needs to relate to God *through* him. He corrects the Corinthians on that: "For as woman came from man, so also man is born of woman." There is not a man alive who has not been born of a woman, including Jesus Christ himself, and who does not owe his existence to her. Even so, above all, is God: "But everything comes from God." This should put an end to squabbles about who owes their existence to whom, who came first, and who takes precedence! Men and women owe their existence to one another, are interdependent, and are on an entirely equal and mutual footing before God.

Then he goes on to ask them a rhetorical question.

> Judge for yourselves: Is it fitting for a woman to pray to God with her head uncovered?

From all we know of Paul and his view of freedom from religious practices for believers, I think by this stage he is hoping and expecting that they will answer "Yes, of course it's appropriate for a woman to pray to God with her head uncovered!"

THE "NATURE OF THINGS"?

The next verse poses a problem for interpreters. On the one hand, we know that in Jewish thinking and some early Christian thinking it wasn't unusual to equate "nature" with God and the way that he has ordered the universe. You could use the word "nature" as a substitute for God. So Paul could have used "nature" in that way, as synonymous with God, and everyone would have understood that. But is it actually true that the "nature of things" (i.e., the way that God has ordered the universe) really teaches us that if a man has long hair it's a disgrace? We certainly don't think that now. Did Paul think that? It's hard for us to tell, as he doesn't use the term "nature" in this precise way anywhere else. So he might have done, but I'm not convinced that he did, and here's why.

It would be very odd if it were Paul who was saying this because *he himself* had long hair while he was in Corinth! In Acts 18:18, Luke makes a reference to Paul cutting his hair when he left Corinth in relation to a vow he took before he went there. Scholars believe that Paul took a vow when he arrived at Corinth, which meant that he only cut his hair after he left. If he had been growing his hair for eighteen months, it would have been about nine inches long—past his shoulders. It's unlikely, first as a Jew, and secondly as a Jew who had probably taken a Nazirite vow, that he really believed long hair on a man was a disgrace.[6] And it seems doubly odd that he would tell *the Corinthians* that long hair on men was against nature when they were the *very same people* among whom he had lived while his own hair was long! They could hardly miss the inconsistency!

The Corinthians, on the other hand, could well have thought that. First of all, it would be likely, given the philosophical thinking that the Corinthians were familiar with, that *they* did see the "nature of things" or what they saw as "natural" as telling them what God had ordained or not. It's not unlikely that the Roman and Greek Corinthians believed that long hair on men was a disgrace, and they had probably told Paul that when he was with them. Maybe they'd even been ashamed of Paul with his long hair! So he turns the tables on them. My view is that he goes on to tease them about one of their own ideas, that the "nature of things" teaches us that men should have short hair, but then in a clever move, uses their own argument against them. *If* you really think that nature of things teaches us something, then surely a woman's "natural" state, her long hair, is her glory. Why would you force her to cover it?

> Does not the very nature of things teach you that if a man
> has long hair, it is a disgrace to him, but that if a woman
> has long hair, it is her glory?

He makes his final point. You will read in the NIV, "For long hair is given to her as a covering." However, the word Paul uses is not "as" but "instead of." Long hair is given to her *instead of* a covering. She doesn't need a head covering because she has her *hair*, the very hair they were threatening to cover or shave off! A woman's hair takes the place of the head covering.

6. The Nazirite vow appears in Numbers 6:1–21. It involved abstaining from grape-related and alcoholic drinks, not cutting one's hair, and keeping ritually clean. It was a way of consecrating oneself and staying close to God.

NO SUCH CUSTOM

He has one last thing to say, which he delivers in a completely uncompromising manner; that is that no-one in any of the other churches has this practice and that they should not go against him and try and divide the church on this issue. It's important to understand the emphatic nature of this final verse. Paul is not messing about.

Some scholars argue that the practice Paul is referring to is just "being divisive" (i.e., we have no such custom of being divisive). I don't believe this is the case, but even if it were to be that, *which* practice is he asking them to agree with him over to prove that they aren't being divisive?! Head coverings for women . . . or not? I think that the custom he's referring to is the practice of putting women in head coverings. We have no such custom, and nor do the churches of God. Whatever we think, because he's so uncompromising, we do need to make a decision about which practice he is referring to.

If we sincerely believe that he's referring to the practice of throwing off head coverings as the custom that we don't practice, of women being bare-headed and men covering their heads, then "Bible-believing Christians" should consider reinstating the practice of head coverings for women when they pray and prophesy in church. After all, he has made the point that this is not a culturally rooted practice, but one that is rooted in creation. However, if we think that he is referring to the practice of making women wear head coverings, and telling the Corinthians that there is no other practice, or no such custom in any other of his churches, then we can finally see that Paul was adamantly opposed to head coverings for women, not just at Corinth, but in *all* his churches.

> If anyone wants to be dangerously divisive about this, we have no such custom—nor do the churches of God.

Here is the passage again, as a conversation, with my own paraphrase, and the Corinthian thought in italics.

1 CORINTHIANS 11:2–16

I praise you for remembering me in everything and for holding to the traditions/teachings, just as I passed them on to you. But I want you to have understood that the head of every man is Christ, and the head of the woman is man, but the head of Christ is God. You say,

> *Every man who prays or prophesies with his head covered dishonors his head. And every woman who prays or prophesies with her head uncovered dishonors her head—it is just as though her head were shaved.*

So if a woman does not cover her head, she should have her hair cut off; and if it is a disgrace for a woman to have her hair cut or shaved off, she should cover her head?!

You've explained to me that

> *a man ought not to cover his head, since he is the image and glory of God; but the woman is the glory of man. For man did not come from woman, but woman from man; neither was man created for woman, but woman for man. For this reason, and because of the angels, the woman ought to have a sign of authority on her head.*

What I am saying to you, though, is that in the Lord, woman is not independent of or separate from man, nor is man independent of or separate from woman. For as woman came from man, so also man is born of woman. But ultimately everything comes from God anyway.

So judge for yourselves: Is it really fitting for a woman to pray to God with her head uncovered? You think that *the very nature of things* teaches you that if a man has long hair, it is a disgrace to him, so then surely if a woman has long hair, it is her glory?! For long hair is given to her in the place of a head covering. If anyone of you wants to be dangerously divisive about this, you should know that we have no such custom—nor do the churches of God.

MAKING SENSE OF THE NON-SENSE

There are so many ways in which the passage now makes sense if we read it in this rhetorical way as an argument *against* head coverings.

1. First, as you can see, the passage takes on its own logic, and the contradictions disappear because they're not contradictions in *Paul's* thought, but contradictions between Paul's teaching and that of certain important Corinthian men.

2. Second, the problems that we have in translation and making sense of certain words ceases to pose a problem because they are not Paul's words. In other words, we don't have to find a reason for why Paul thinks that women should wear head coverings because women are the glory of man and "because of the angels" because he never thought that in the first place.

3. Third, Paul's rejection of head coverings for women, on the grounds that they are equal to men and that their hair, which is their natural glory, is covering enough is entirely in line with the rest of Paul's thought in the letter and in other letters, most specifically spelled out in Galatians.

4. Fourth, it makes sense of why Paul is telling them that there is no such custom (the wearing of head coverings for women) in any other church.

5. Fifth, it is in line with other passages in Corinthians where it is recognized that Paul is responding to the letter from the Corinthians, repeating their own argument to them, and then going on to refute it.

6. Sixth, and finally, this reading accords with the view noted above that Paul is using this letter to address with some force certain ungodly practices that some in the church have implemented in his absence.

In the next chapter, we'll look the deeper complications that we face if we want to insist that the *whole* passage is all Paul's own thought.

3

Whose Image? Whose Glory?

We've begun to highlight a few of the problems in our verses. In the next two chapters I want to go a bit deeper into some specific concepts that emerge from 1 Corinthians 11:2–16 and have a huge impact on the way that women are treated in the church. I will show you some of the really difficult issues with these ideas in 1 Corinthians 11 in order to explain why these verses cannot be taken in a straightforward manner to keep women out of leadership.

In this chapter, we'll look in more detail at 1 Corinthians 11:7–9 and the concepts of image and glory, and in the next chapter we'll explore what Paul might have meant by using the language of "head" in relation to man and woman in 11:3. These ideas of image, glory, and headship are crucial to the passage and are important to the church because they lie behind a lot of the theology of men and women in many churches.

There's an assumption (a fair one) that these verses are telling us something significant about men and women and how they relate, but what we'll see is that they are much more complex than some people like to admit, which makes applying them to contemporary situations almost impossible. Imagining that you can just gloss over these complications is not being true to the text, as we will see.

THE IMAGE AND GLORY OF MAN

In the NIV, you will read 11:7–10 as this:

> 7 A man ought not to cover his head, since he is the image and glory of God; but woman is the glory of man. 8 For man did not come from woman, but woman from man; 9 neither was man created for woman, but woman for man. 10 It is for this reason that a woman ought to have authority over her own head, because of the angels.

Let me show you though how this has been translated differently in another version in order to give a different impression. If you look at the NRSV, you will see that the word for "glory" has been translated as "reflection" and not as glory. In addition to this, the editors have added the word "symbol" to verse 10. So it reads like this:

> 7 For a man ought not to have his head veiled, since he is the image and *reflection* of God; but woman is the reflection of man. 8 Indeed, man was not made from woman, but woman from man. 9 Neither was man created for the sake of woman, but woman for the sake of man. 10 For this reason a woman ought to have *a symbol* of authority on her head, because of the angels. (NRSV)

The word for glory in Greek is *doxa*. The editors of the NRSV have decided to translate this word, *doxa*, as "reflection" and not "glory." However, if you look up translations of *doxa*, "reflection" is not given as a possible translation for the Greek word. You can see that this choice of word changes the meaning considerably and you could say, it's not what the text says. The editors know this so they have put a footnote by "reflection" to say "or glory," acknowledging the alternative translation and letting you know about it. But how many people read the footnotes? In verse 15, where *doxa* appears again, they translate it as glory, but with no footnote saying that it could be translated as "reflection." I imagine they have dropped the word "glory" and inserted "reflection" here in verse 7 as the idea that men alone are the "glory" of God sounds strange and wrong, as I will explain below.

What about the other decision that they make in the RSV? They've put an interpretation of what the head covering might mean by adding the phrase "symbol of authority." Again, that's not really what the text says, so we have to ask ourselves what they were trying to tell us by adding this idea of a "symbol"? I think the editors are trying to make it sound as if the woman has her *own* authority when she wears her head covering. This is the opposite of sounding like she's being forced into wearing it in order to have permission to pray to God.

So that is a little snapshot of how differently these verses are interpreted by different people and how differently you would understand them depending on what version of the Bible you had and how it had been explained to you. Throughout the history of the church, people have found these verses quite challenging because of what they appear to say about men and women.

We've already noted that the reasons spelled out in verses 7–10 are the reasons given for women to wear head coverings and for men to take theirs off. I think that these are the reasons that the Corinthians have given to Paul for making women wear head coverings, but other people still insist that this is what Paul himself thinks.

THE PERPLEXITY OF PAUL'S VOICE

Let's imagine that it is Paul and see where that takes us, because it's only if we think that he really wrote this and believes it that it becomes challenging.

Let's read the verses again.

> 7 A man ought not to cover his head, since he is the image and glory of God; but woman is the glory of man. 8 For man did not come from woman, but woman from man; 9 neither was man created for woman, but woman

for man. 10 It is for this reason that a woman ought to
have authority over her own head, because of the angels.

I often ask the students in my class how these verses strike them,
what they think they are saying, or how they make them feel. I
won't give you all the answers that they give me, but I'd like you to
do the same. What do you think these verses are saying? If this is
what Paul thought about men and women, how do they strike you?
How do they make you feel? I don't know how you have answered
those questions, but I'll tell you a bit of how they've been understood through the ages and how scholars have tried to understand
them.

MAN IS THE IMAGE AND GLORY OF GOD; WOMAN IS NOT

The majority of readers of these verses think that this is saying
that man and *not woman* is the image and glory of God, and that
woman has a glory that comes from her relationship with man. It
seems reasonably clear that the idea in verses 7–9 is that image-
bearing and glory-bearing belong primarily to the male because
of a man's relation to God. Man or men are the image and glory
of God directly, and women have a different status, and a different
relation to God and to his glory. They are the glory of men because,
as the writer claims, man did not come from woman, but woman
from man, and man was not created for woman, but woman for
man. It sounds as if man as the original creation was created for
God, to bear his image and his glory, and woman was created
with the sole purpose of being related to the male. For this reason,
she has a derived or reflected glory (maybe that's why the NRSV
translates the word, "reflection"?). Her glory is hers because of her
relationship with the man.

The problem is that this account quite clearly contradicts the
other creation accounts in the Bible that tell us a different story
about men and women. This account also makes it sound as if
women really don't have their own place before God and have to

come to him with some kind of go-between (a man) and that the head covering is the symbol of that. But why would that be the case? And as Paul changes the story a few sentences later, why would he have said it in the first place?

LOVING OR HATING PAUL?

Most Christians who hold the Bible as authoritative and the word of God want to think that these verses make sense and that they tell us something valuable about men and women. They respect the Bible and respect Paul, so they look for meaning that will help us understand better what he might have meant. On the other hand, there are people who don't care about doing that. It might be that they don't actually have much respect for Paul, or maybe also the Bible, and so they don't mind if Paul comes across as inconsistent, women-hating, or muddled. Or it may be that they *do* have respect for the Bible, and because of this they don't think that we have to make it always sound consistent if it clearly isn't. For whatever reasons, there are people who are not invested in trying to make Paul sound good. If you did want to make him sound good though, you would need these verses to make sense in their own context, in the context of Paul's thought, and in the context of the wider message of the Bible. Can we make them do that?

A STORY ABOUT CREATION?

Many people simply assume that the reasons given for head coverings in these verses are rooted in the creation story in some way, but it's not what the creation stories in Genesis actually say.

There are two creation stories in Genesis. The first is in Genesis 1:26–27.

> 26 Then God said, "Let us make mankind in our image, in our likeness, so that they may rule over the fish in the sea and the birds in the sky, over the livestock and all the

wild animals, and over all the creatures that move along the ground."

> 27 So God created mankind in his own image,
>   in the image of God he created them;
>   male and female he created them.

The second one occurs in Genesis 2:7 and Genesis 2:19–24.

> 7 Then the LORD God formed a man from the dust of the ground and breathed into his nostrils the breath of life, and the man became a living being.
>
> 19 Now the LORD God had formed out of the ground all the wild animals and all the birds in the sky. He brought them to the man to see what he would name them; and whatever the man called each living creature, that was its name. 20 So the man gave names to all the livestock, the birds in the sky and all the wild animals.
>
> But for Adam no suitable helper was found. 21 So the LORD God caused the man to fall into a deep sleep; and while he was sleeping, he took one of the man's ribs and then closed up the place with flesh. 22 Then the LORD God made a woman from the rib he had taken out of the man, and he brought her to the man.
>
> 23 The man said,
> "This is now bone of my bones
>   and flesh of my flesh;
> she shall be called 'woman',
> for she was taken out of man."
>
> 24 That is why a man leaves his father and mother and is united to his wife, and they become one flesh.

GENESIS 1 OR GENESIS 2?

It is true, if we ignore the account in Genesis 1 and just focus on Genesis 2 we can say that it makes sense to claim that woman "comes from" man. That's why people assume that verse 7 has some kind of foundation in Genesis. The problem with this is that then we'd have to explain why we were going to ignore Genesis 1.

In our first story, God makes male *and female* in his own image, not just man. That's our first problem.

Secondly, we'd have to ignore the story further on. If you read on to Genesis 4:1 you'll find that when Eve gives birth to Cain she rejoices, "With the help of the LORD I have brought forth a man." Even in the early stories of creation, woman brings forth man— and then *man comes from woman*. And even Paul continues on to say this in 1 Corinthians 11:12, "Nevertheless, in the Lord woman is not independent of man, nor is man independent of woman. For as woman came from man, so also man is born of woman. But everything comes from God."

We looked at verse 11 in the last chapter, making the point that the word we read as "nevertheless" is actually a much stronger word than that and signals a change of direction in someone's thinking. So most people recognize that it sounds here as if he's changed his mind in some way. Which view is closest to what he really thinks? If you want Paul to make sense, you won't want Paul to hold contradictory views, you'll try and make it sound as if you can just hold these two views together "in tension." Both can be true in some way. Does this work?

TENSION OR CONTRADICTION?

Personally, I can't see that the two views can be held in tension. In my view, once you've made the second statement, that men and women are interdependent and that everything comes from God, it cancels out the first. It sounds to me as if Paul is overriding the first view with the second, and the second is clearly the more important, and the more correct!

Some people like to explain this as two views in tension by saying that the first view is how Paul sees men and women at creation, and the second view is how he sees men and women "in the Lord," almost as if they are two biblical views from different perspectives referring to different eras in the Bible—BC and AD. The trouble with this is that in verses 11–12 he isn't just referring to how men and women relate "in the Lord," he is referring back to creation there as well. In Genesis 4:1 we read that men "come" from women. They're born from them and they always have been. Verses 11–12 are part of the creation story as well. So, are verses 11–12 a contradiction of what he's said in verses 7–9, or is it a correction, or is it a kind of modification of his views?

What I'm saying is that you can't make such strong statements about man being God's image and glory and woman being the glory of man because she comes from him, she was made from him, and she was made for him, and then argue for interdependence without it looking like you're backtracking. It sounds as if Paul's changed his mind. You as the reader have to decide. Is he just holding two views at once or did he write something and then correct it rather than just leaving it out *or* is he answering the Corinthians' misguided views?

PAUL'S VIEWS OF CREATION

Let's dig a bit deeper. Not only do our verses not really describe the creation stories in Genesis as a whole, but there is nowhere in the OT that we can find a basis for claiming that (a) man *alone* is the "image" of God (it is always assumed that men and women together are the image of God) or (b) that man is the image and *glory* of God. In Genesis 1, it's man and woman together who are the image and *likeness* of God, so this phrase is an adaptation of the early texts in two important ways. First, it refers only to the man. Second, it claims that man alone is the image and *glory*. Psalm 8 does refer to the crowning of humanity with glory and honor (Ps 8:5), so maybe there's a link there, but the role of ruling also referred to in the psalm is assigned to both men and women together, not solely to the man. How does that square with the ideas we find in 11:7–9?

WHICH "MAN" IS GOD'S GLORY?

A further problem is which "man" is Paul referring to when he says that man is the image and glory of God? Is it *all* men, or all *Christian* men, or all Christian *husbands?* This has confused interpreters. John Chrysostom, for instance, a fourth-century bishop, thought it was ridiculous to make this claim of *all* men and applied it only to Christian men in relation to Christian women, but then does that mean only husbands and wives or all Christian men in relation to all Christian women? This is not quite so clear, even in Chrysostom. However, if it's just husbands and wives, it does appear to let Paul off the hook in some way, especially if you think that *Christian* husbands who have Christ as their "head" are given his glory and image. But it doesn't really say that. The "plain sense" reading of the text is that it seems to be referring to a creation story. Most scholars raise all these questions in one form or another. Why does Paul claim that man and *not* woman is the image of God? That's what it sounds like, but how can we explain it?

CHANGING VIEWS: OLD AND NEW

In the past, most readers of the Bible—especially male readers and scholars—were okay with the idea that men were created with some kind of superior status to women, so 1 Corinthians 11:7–9 simply told them something they already believed to be true. It was acceptable to read these verses as they stand, implying that women should wear a head covering because they have a different, and lower, status to men. Chrysostom, whom I mentioned above, saw the bare head on the man as a symbol of his rule and a head covering on the woman as a symbol of her subjection to man. He believed that Paul thought for a man to be covered was wrong because it meant that he had fallen into the place of inferiority that rightly belonged to the woman. Similarly, if the woman was to go uncovered, that was a sign that she had ideas above her station and was taking the man's rightful place. It was a gross disruption of both the society's and God's order.[1]

The idea of the natural or God-given superiority of men over women that can clearly be taken out of the first half of our passage (vv. 4–10) has featured in most readings of these verses throughout the ages. As time has passed, however, this "plain sense" reading becomes more and more of an embarrassment and we find scholars trying to avoid the meaning one way or another. What I found interesting in my own research was realizing that this wasn't just a modern phenomenon. People think we've become embarrassed by the idea of the superiority of men and inferiority of women because of our culture, or more directly because of feminism perhaps. But Augustine, a direct contemporary of Chrysostom, refused to read this text as saying that women were in reality inferior or subordinate to men, and came up with an extremely elaborate explanation of what Paul must have meant by making women wear head coverings.

AUGUSTINE'S VIEW

Augustine thinks it's peculiar that Paul seems to imply that man and not woman is the image of God because that's not what it says in Genesis 1:27. He asks why it seems as if Paul the apostle is contradicting Genesis and goes on to explain what he thinks Paul actually meant in order to prove that he doesn't contradict Scripture at all.[2] The problem for us is that Augustine's argument is not at all a "plain sense" reading and makes no sense for the way that we understand the nature of human being in the modern world. In a nutshell, Augustine argues that women and men together symbolize the entire image of God, but that women, in their female bodies, symbolize the lower, dishonorable parts of the image that is found in the human psyche or mind. However, he's adamant that they only *symbolize* the lower and inferior parts. No one would

1. Chrysostom, *Homilies on the Epistles of Paul to the Corinthians*, 26.4.
2. See Augustine, *On the Trinity*, XII.3.10.

ever think that they really were lower and more dishonorable! In other words, he doesn't apply it in a concrete way to the subordination of women, but that's his explanation as to why women should be covered up. You can read his argument in chapter 12 of *On the Trinity*, but be prepared for a complicated journey in thinking as you follow his logic. I enjoy reading his work though because he's so insistent that if we don't understand this passage as *purely* symbolic and not at all literal then the passage is pointless!

So you see, it doesn't mean that if we take offense or struggle with the ideas in these verses that it's just because we're modern, or just because we've been affected by feminism, or just because we're trying to avoid the bits of the Bible that we don't like. This was identified as a problem for readers very early on.

THE PLAIN SENSE READING

There is a plain sense reading of verses 7–9, and that is that women were created in some kind of inferior and dependent position to men. This becomes very clear if we think that Paul is enforcing head coverings because the head covering is worn to make up for a natural lack and difference in women. It's quite shocking to read through one commentary after another that seems to accept the idea that Paul really thought that women were somehow naturally inferior to men or somehow less glorious, and so needed something to compensate for that. This is made even more problematic by the fact that verses 11–12 contradict this, straight after it, and in reality are a more Christian picture of men and women together both in creation and in the Lord.

NOT PAUL, BUT HIS OPPONENTS

In my reading, verses 7–9 are not Paul's ideas, but the Corinthians ideas, and they encapsulate the main reasons that the Corinthians have for making women wear head coverings in worship. These are the reasons they gave to Paul when he challenged them on it. They are interesting and powerful reasons.

WHAT CREATION TELLS US

What we see is a corrupted creation story used to keep women in a particular place in relation to men—in need of a sign of "authority." What is going on here is a blended account of the two creation stories that has been manipulated for a particular purpose. First it places woman in a particular place in relation to God and also to man, which then redefines her identity as primarily rooted in her relationship to man rather than to God. Second it writes her out of her shared role of image and likeness (and glory) bearer, *and* as the creator and bearer of man that we find in Genesis.

As this has become more and more embarrassing, some scholars try to excuse Paul or to let him off the hook. Some claim that what he really meant is that women are the "crowning glory" of creation. Others say that women and men are in some kind of mutual glorying relationship; men are glorified by women and women are glorified by men. But this is not an obvious reading of the text. The text is about the fact that men are acting shamefully if they don't accept their glorious status before Christ, and women are acting shamefully if they don't acknowledge that their glory is in man. Even when scholars are trying to gloss over the embarrassment of these verses, they still have to admit that the lack of a woman's own glory means that she needs to wear something on her head and that if she doesn't comply with the rules, there's a punishment in view! This is not very mutual.

IN THE LORD

I have a feeling that many people actually just ignore verses 7–10 because of what immediately follows in verses 11–16. Rather than focusing on the glaring contradiction between the first and second section, they simply focus on Paul's thought in verses 11–16, which suddenly becomes much safer and more familiar. It's easy for us to do this because of the break at verse 11 that we've studied. It kind of says to us, "But this is what I really think . . . ."

THE CORINTHIAN MAN'S GLORY

What happens if we say that verses 7–10 express Corinthian thought and not Paul's? First, it becomes much clearer why there is a corrupted form of Genesis 1:26–27, which consistently perturbs readers. The Corinthian prophetic leaders and teachers who claim that they "have the word of God" are teaching that men are the image and glory of God, and that women are merely the image and glory of man. This serves as the perfect rationale for the subordination of women and the superiority of men.

This theology of glory in a congregation that is most concerned with who has the glory and how it's manifest has taken over at Corinth. It's obscured any sense of what Paul taught them about what it means for both men and women to be in Christ. This, and their view of the angels watching and judging them in their worship, acts as their theological reason for their view that head coverings for women were honoring for God, men, and the angels. In addition to this, this would also serve as the perfect reason not just for head coverings, but for keeping women silent before their husbands, as they must adopt a subordinate role. This too then makes sense of 1 Corinthians 14:33–36, as we saw in Bushnell's reading.

SUMMARY

It should be clear by now that there are no *cultural* reasons given in these verses for the shame that an uncovered woman and a covered man creates. The shame is caused by a disrespect of the order in a particular view of creation, and the disapproval that this will give rise to; the disapproval comes from God and the angels, not from society around them.

The reasons given are not to do with the worry that women will look like men or lesbians and that men will look like women or homosexuals, as some scholars claim. This is not simply about respecting gender difference in the culture around them. The dilemma is this: if this is what Paul really thinks about men and women, then how would that apply today? The only real application of these verses, if we think that Paul wrote them, and we think that he is an authoritative voice for the church, is that women should wear head coverings in church when they pray and prophesy, as an authorizing sign that they may take part in the worship. Let's now turn to people's views of Paul's views on "headship," which are mainly taken from the key verse, 1 Corinthians 11:3.

4

Where and Who Is My Head?

In this chapter we look at the question of "headship," a word that doesn't appear in the Bible, but that has its origins in 1 Corinthians 11:3:

> But I want you to realize that the head of every man is Christ, and the head of the woman is man, and the head of Christ is God.

We find similar references to this idea in Ephesians, which we'll come on to at the end of the chapter. The idea that a man is the "head" of a woman has been interpreted in many ways. Let's look at this verse to see what it tells us about this idea of women, men, and Christ all having a "head" and God, Christ, and man being a "head" of someone while woman is the "head" of no one.[1]

THE CONTEXT AND STRUCTURE OF 11:3

Before Paul writes about the "head," he says to them, "I praise you for remembering me in everything and for holding to the traditions just as I passed them on to you." A lot of people notice that

---

1. For more detail on the debate about *kephale*/head, see Peppiatt, *Women and Worship*, 85–97.

this sounds strange given that Paul is about to go on to rebuke them and correct them about head coverings. In other places, when Paul corrects the Corinthians he either begins by saying, "Do you not know . . ." (3:16; 5:6; 6:2, 3, 9, 15, 16, 19; 9:13, 34) or "I do not wish you to be ignorant . . ." (10:1; 12:1). The fact that he begins in a different way should be a clue for us that he is communicating something different here from just a straightforward rebuke or correction. Some people even wonder whether he's being sarcastic, but I don't think so. What were the traditions that they were actually holding onto that he was praising them for?

It seems that Paul is being entirely genuine in praising them for holding on to some of his traditions about the head, but it also seems that he needs to correct them because they're not exactly right in what they are teaching. This is what is going on in 11:3. If we translated the beginning of verse 3 literally it would read, "But I want you to have understood . . . ." So it seems like he's saying, "Well done for holding on to the traditions that I passed on to you, but I wanted you to have understood that . . . ." What is it that he wishes they had understood or wants them to understand now? We read three things:

- the head of every man is Christ
- the head of the woman is man
- the head of Christ is God

The word that Paul uses to link the three pairings can be translated either as "and" or "but." You can see in the NIV that the editors have translated it as "but" in the first instance, and then "and" after that. The fact that they use "but" between verses 2–3 (*"But I want you to understand . . ."*) means that they too think that Paul is praising the Corinthians for one thing (holding on to some traditions), *but* then correcting them on the particulars of this issue.

Paul needs to correct them and so puts the "head" talk in context. And the context is that *"the head of Christ is God."* We know that this is the most important claim in this sentence because it comes last and is the climax of the sentence. This is the key pairing at the end that shapes how we should think of everything else.

The fact that God is the head of Christ is the pivotal theological principle and the truth that we mustn't lose sight of when we're discussing anything to do with "headship." This is why he puts this last—for emphasis. Let's read it again.

> But I want you to have understood that the head of every man is Christ, and the head of woman is man, *but* the head of Christ is God.

This relationship defines every other. For this reason, we should work first at trying to understand what Paul might have meant by calling God the "head" of Christ and then that will give us a clue to how we might be able to think about the rest.

FOLLOWING A TRAIL

There are two ways that we can try to find out what a certain Greek word means in a certain context in the NT. The first is to find all the other instances of that word in the rest of the Bible and see what it means in those contexts. The second is to study other texts that were written around the same time and see if there's a particular meaning, or a way that it was being used, which makes sense of the word that we are studying. If we do this with *kephale*, the word for "head," we find that the word had multiple meanings at the time that Paul was using it. The meanings range from a literal, physical head (which is the normal meaning) to source or origin, first principle, ruler, one in authority, crown, completion, the coping of a wall, the capital of a column, and still other uses.

Because Paul uses the same word for three different relationships, in order to make a decision about which meaning we might choose for verse 3, we then have to look at our own context and choose one that will make sense in all three pairings. If the same word is used to describe the relationship of God to Christ, Christ to man, and man to woman, then what might it mean? This is the challenge. The truth is that we struggle to find one meaning that is going to apply to all three equally, so I will explain why that is and what possible solutions there might be.

GOD AND CHRIST

Let's start with the God/Christ relation because that is our key pairing. First, we have to rule out "physical head," which was the most normal meaning of the word *kephale*, as that clearly doesn't work. God is not the physical head of Christ. Another quite popular way of understanding "head" in evangelical circles is to mean "ruler" or even "one in authority" like you might talk about the "head" of a school or an organization. This doesn't work either and was rejected early on in the church because even if you thought that Christ could rule a man and a man could rule a woman, it can't be applied to God and Christ. God is not the "ruler" of Christ or the one in authority over him as this would make Christ subordinate to God and as if they were on a different plane. The early church had to keep making the point that Christ *is* God, and is therefore of one substance with him and equal to him. Despite this reading of ruler or one in authority being rejected early on, it has recently been mistakenly reinstated. Christ *is* God, and has been given all authority in heaven and earth.

SOURCE OR ORIGIN

How about source or origin? This is a popular choice, but it too has its problems. It works quite well for the God/Christ relation. It even works quite well for the man/woman pairing if we focus only on the Genesis 2 story of creation and take it to mean something more literal about woman coming from man. However, it unravels in the Christ/man relation. Christ is not really the source of man alone in the same way that God could be understood to be the source of Christ or man the source of woman. When "man" is taken out of something it is not out of Christ, but out of the dust of the earth. Moreover, the whole Godhead created humanity, male and female.

FIRST PRINCIPLE

We could say that God is the "first principle" of Christ. This is an ancient concept meaning the principle from which something else is derived. It would have a similar meaning to source or origin, but without the idea of one necessarily existing before another. Although it sounds as if we might be saying one thing comes first and gives rise to another, this expression wouldn't have been understood like that when Paul was writing. If one thing were the "first principle" of another it would have told the readers more about what the two things share in terms of their essence and how they're related, than their sequence. It certainly doesn't have any overtones of "authority" or "ruling," which is helpful and so it is quite an attractive option.

However, it's still not without its problems if we try and apply it in the same way to all three pairs. Christ is not derived from God in the same fashion that man might be derived from Christ and woman is from man in Genesis 2. Christ is not created (because that would make him a creature and not God) but rather what we call "eternally begotten." We use this phrase to try and describe the Father/Son relation in the Godhead between two persons of God who share the same essence. Christ has always existed with the Father and the Father couldn't be the eternal Father without having always had an eternal Son. So it would be wrong to imply that one came first before the other; this would imply that Christ is not God in the same way that God is God and this would lead us into error. In addition to this, people like to say that this verse is about the Trinity, but it's not really about the Trinity as the Spirit doesn't even get a mention! What we do know is that the Son is eternally begotten, has always been with and from the Father and was not born/made like a real physical Son. So how is God his "head"?

CHRIST AND MAN

How about man to Christ? What is that relation? First of all, man and woman are created and belong to the creaturely realm. We have two stories of creation and in neither one does it imply that man is "taken" from Christ. In one, God creates man and woman together in his image. In the other, man is taken from the dust of the earth, not from Christ, the head. You see the difficulty of finding a word that means the same for all three relationships.

From very early on, scholars have realized this problem. John Chrysostom made some helpful comments on this verse on precisely this issue of not being able to find an exact parallel between each pairing. Steve Holmes translates Chrysostom's comment like this:

> So, we shouldn't use the same arguments about our human existence and God's divine existence, even if we use similar language. We have to recognise God's transcendence—God is so great! If they [interpreters] don't admit this, they end up with all sorts of absurdities—God is the head of Christ, and Christ is the head of man, and man of the woman; if we take "head" in the same sense every time, then the Son will be as distant from the Father as we are from the Son—and the woman will be as far from us as we are from the divine Word, and what the Son is to the Father, we are to the Son, and the woman is to the man. Who could accept all that?[2]

What Chrysostom is saying is that because the relationship of God to Christ is so radically different from any relationship of Christ to male human beings or male human beings to female human beings that we can't actually imagine that this one word can be applied in *exactly the same way* in each of the relationships. We can't say that man is related to Christ like Christ is to God, so what does it mean to use the word "head" for all three?

2. Holmes, "John Chrysostom," Shored Fragments.

KNOWING WHAT WE CAN'T SAY

I often say to my students that the way we work out what we *can* say about the meaning of a text or the nature of God is by beginning with what we *can't* say. This is so often the way that scholars and theologians work. So far, we've looked at what we can't say. So what might we be able to say that's positive about this word, *kephale*, or head? We can conclude that it's used in three similar but different ways, and that it tells us something about how one thing stands in relation to another, rather than telling us much about how that relationship functions. Let's map that idea on to our text in context.

WHAT WE CAN SAY

First of all, it seems as if Paul is referring to something that he has taught them. This would make sense as he uses similar language in Ephesians about Christ relating to the church as a head to a body in a similar fashion to the way that he sees husbands related to wives. It would make more sense then if we first understood *kephale* language when used by Paul only in relation to husbands and wives, as in Ephesians 5, rather than to all men and all women. Have a look at the RSV translation of this verse and you'll see that the editors of the RSV have already decided that this is how it should be translated. They just use "husband." This solves our problem of which "man" he might be referring to in verse 3, because it doesn't make sense to see it as all men. It is also an acceptable translation as the Greek word for man can also mean husband and the Greek word for woman can also mean wife.

If this were the case we could draw some conclusions that in Paul's mind his teaching on God/Christ, Christ/husband, and husband/wife is something to do with the idea that each one is connected to one another like a physical head is connected to a physical body, and thus forms an inseparable unit in a similar way.

First of all, even if this is along the right lines, we shouldn't get too carried away here with the metaphor in terms of how we understand marriage. It's not so encouraging that the wife is left at the end of the line as *kephale* of no-one. It seems as if she has no direct connection with Christ, and is now connected to God through her husband. In addition to this, it leaves unmarried women without a *kephale* and therefore unconnected to the Godhead. Is this what Paul meant to convey? Not really. How do we know?

PAUL'S VIEWS ON MARRIAGE

In terms of the marriage relation, Paul has some of the most radical teaching that you can find in the ancient world and it comes a few chapters before 1 Corinthians 11. I find it interesting that so many men choose to interpret a few verses in Ephesians as a blueprint for a marriage in order to say that a Christian husband has authority over his wife, who in turn, they say, should be submissive and subordinate to her husband, but then completely ignore 1 Corinthians 7. In 1 Corinthians 7:4, Paul tells the Corinthian wives that just as their husbands have authority over their bodies, they too have authority over their husbands' bodies.

> For the wife does not have authority over her own body,
> but the husband does; likewise the husband does not
> have authority over his own body, but the wife does.

Here is where Paul actually uses the word "authority"—which you won't find in 1 Corinthians 11 or in Ephesians 5—and it's *entirely mutual!* The idea that a wife would have *any* authority over her husband in sexual matters was unheard of in Paul's time. Hays writes this about 1 Corinthians 7:4, "In contrast to a patriarchal culture that would assume a one-way hierarchical ordering of the husband's authority over the wife, Paul carefully prescribes *mutual submission.* Neither marriage partner controls his or her own body: in the marriage covenant, one surrenders authority over one's own body to the spouse."[3] The emphasis on mutuality here is striking.

So, first of all we can see that the "head" picture is not to be associated with hierarchy, authority, and subordination because

3. Hays, *The Moral Vision*, 1491.

that doesn't work with God/Christ and it doesn't work with man/woman and it doesn't even work with husband/wife. Does Ephesians help us to work out what it might mean as this is the other place where we find the language of "head"?

EPHESIANS 5

In Ephesians 5:22–33, Paul talks about the church's relationship to Christ by using the metaphor of a marriage. People like to say that this picture definitely supports the idea of a submissive and even subordinate wife, but again, it's really not that simple. First of all, when Paul begins this teaching on the church, he has just told the whole church at Ephesus that they should "Submit to one another out of reverence to Christ" (5:21). Secondly, remember that Christ is the "head" of the entire church made up of men, women, and children. There is only one "head" of and in the church and that is Christ. The rest of us make up the body. All men are together with all women and all children in the body of Christ and we all have one head—Christ.

Having said that, it is interesting that Paul chooses only one particular role in the Christian church to illustrate the way in which Christ relates to his church. He chooses the role of a *Christian* husband, which is radically different from the role of a normal husband of his time. The characteristics of this husband are that he sacrifices his life to the point of death for his wife, giving up everything for her and her salvation and flourishing.

Why is it that men focus on a picture of submission of wives, which would not have sounded radical for Paul's audience, and ignore the bombshell that he dropped on the listening husbands? Effectively he is denying them the rights and the powers that their society would have assumed were theirs. Their lot is to be identified with a crucified Savior who gave himself up for the ones he adored, and to give up their lives for their wives.

THE WOMAN IS THE *KEPHALE* OF NO ONE

It is true that a wife is the *kephale* of no one. We can't get around that. I don't believe, however, in the light of his other teaching, that Paul intended for this to be a demeaning or belittling doctrine for wives. Let's go back to our ultimate pair. God is the *kephale* of Christ. I think that Paul had in mind something to do with union, identity, and destiny. Christ is one with God. A Christian husband must stay one with Christ. A Christian wife is one with her husband. This is Paul's vision for the closest of all possible relations. This means then that our identities are bound up with one another. We can't break off the union. We belong to one another. We have an interdependence and a depth of shared identity that goes beyond anything that we know in the world. It isn't that surprising, knowing the place that men and husbands had in Paul's society, that when he was trying to find an illustration to explain the love that Christ has for his church, he chose the picture of a Christian marriage, positioning the husband as the *kephale* and the wife as the body. But we cannot lose sight of the fact that this is how he chose to explain Christ's unending covenant *love* and sacrifice for the church, and nothing else.

BUT GOD IS THE HEAD OF CHRIST

So, in 11:3 Paul agrees with them that he had taught them that Christ is the head of a husband and a husband is the head of the wife. I think that the Corinthians had used this as an excuse to exclude and silence the wives, unless those wives wore a sign of authority. This is emphatically *not* what Paul had intended, so he adds a crucial qualifying clause—*God is the head of Christ*. Why is this so important? He explains it all in 11:11–12, "Nevertheless, in the Lord woman is not independent of man, nor is man independent of woman. For as woman came from man, so also man is born of woman. But everything comes from God." This is important because God will be all in all. *All* are from God and *all* will return to God and God will be all in all, as Paul reiterates in

3:23, 11:12, and 15:28. The Corinthian men thought they had a special glorious place in relation to Christ, which gave them authority over the women. Paul is correcting them, reminding them that even Christ, with all of them, men and women, will be taken up into God.

Before we leave this topic, I want to make one more point about the language of the "body" that is related to the concept of the "head" in 1 Corinthians.

YOU ARE THE "BODY" OF CHRIST

At the beginning of 1 Corinthians we discover that Paul is addressing the distressing reality that the Corinthian church is deeply divided. I think that Paul refers back to his language of "head" in verse 3 because he's concerned that his original teaching has been adopted and then corrupted by the Corinthians. Perhaps a group of spiritually gifted men have begun to claim that they are the ones who are now like the glorious Christ. They've become domineering and divisive, and they've begun to implement practices aimed at controlling and/or silencing the women and the wives.

In chapter 12, Paul uses the language of the "body," and specifically the body of Christ in order to describe the Corinthians' situation. He paints a certain picture for them as to how they should behave with one another. Chapter 12 is a window into Paul's thought on the nature of the Christian church and how it should operate, but is also significant within the letter itself as it develops the theme of the language of the body. Through the metaphor of the physical body, Paul exhorts the congregation to elevate respect, love, interdependence, and care for one another over charismatic gifts or "roles." Not only this, but the overriding message of chapter 12 is that those who see themselves as more important and more worthy of honor should instead be honoring the "inferior," the "lowest," and the "least."

Paul's teaching here is not simply that they should be honoring those who are perceived to be inferior, but that there is a God-ordained reversal of status in the body of Christ: "But *God has so adjusted the body*, giving the greater honor to the inferior part." What is the purpose of God having done this? That "there may be no discord in the body, but that the members may have the same care for one another. If one member suffers, all suffer together; if one member is honored/glorified, all rejoice together" (vv. 24–26).

Thus, Paul sets the context for the language of "head" within his picture of the "body" as well as in his theology of God/Christ. First, he warns those who perceive themselves to be in the position of the "head," that they may never say to any other part of the body, "I have no need of you." But second, and far more radically, Paul claims that those who are more "important" must devote themselves to honoring the "dishonorable" parts in the knowledge that those members are the ones who are given the highest honor by God himself. There's no doubt that women, and especially slave women would have been those people at the bottom of the pile.

In our final chapter, we'll look at Paul's big picture to see what light that sheds on these topics.

5

Paul and the Bigger Picture

One of the last topics I want to cover is Paul and the bigger picture. Here we'll see that his overall worldview and his attitudes toward women in general create countless problems for those who want to say that the ideas in 11:4–10 belong to Paul. In this chapter we'll look at:

- What are some of the big ideas that motivated Paul in his ministry?

- What was the "good news" that Paul was so willing to live and die for?

- What happens when we die to ourselves in baptism and rise again in Christ?

- What did it mean for men and women to become "new creations" in Christ?

- What should a cross-shaped, Spirit-filled community look like, according to Paul? How does this fit with the theology of shame and honor, glory, and inferiority and superiority that we find in the first half of our passage?

PAUL AND THE "GOOD NEWS"

Paul uses many pictures in his letters to describe what happened on the cross and in Jesus' death and resurrection that saved humanity: forgiveness, freedom, sacrifice, justification, deliverance, and redemption are just some of the ideas that come up in his letters. But one of the central pictures that he uses is *reconciliation*. The cross means peacemaking among enemies and the restoration of friendship. You can find this theme in many places in his letters. First, humanity is reconciled to God by Jesus' death; we have peace with God and become his sons and daughters. This then means we can be reconciled with one another (become one in Christ), and that we can then take the message of reconciliation out to the world (2 Cor 5:11–21; Eph 2:14–18; Col 1:19–21). If we want to understand what he meant when he described the cross as the means of reconciliation we should ask what this picture of reconciliation might look like in real life and real relationships? Did Paul have anything in mind? If so, what was it?

There's a lot of evidence in Paul's letters that he did know what he thought this reconciliation should look like, and that he did think it should have an impact on real relationships, especially the relationships of Jews to gentiles, freed men and women to their slaves, and men to women. These are the three key sets of relationships that he singles out to comment on in Galatians 3:27–28 where he makes the point that being baptized as a Christian clothes us with Christ, sets us free to be children of God, and makes us all co-equal heirs of all of God's promises. Why does he choose these three pairs: Jew/gentile, slave/free, male/female? For an answer to that, let's turn first to Ephesians 2.

Take some time to read Ephesians 2.

You'll have noticed our theme of peace and reconciliation especially in verses 14–18:

> For he himself is our peace, who has made the two
> groups one and has destroyed the barrier, the dividing

wall of hostility, by setting aside in his flesh the law with its commands and regulations. His purpose was to create in himself one new humanity out of the two, thus making peace, and in one body to reconcile both of them to God through the cross, by which he put to death their hostility. He came and preached peace to you who were far away and peace to those who were near. For through him we both have access to the Father by one Spirit.

THE GOSPEL TO THE GENTILES

Paul says here that God's purpose was to create in himself (in Christ) *one new humanity* out of two races that had been set against each other for as long as anyone could remember. Jews did not mix with gentiles and vice versa. According to Jews, gentiles were "unclean" and would have been excluded both from Jewish worship and from their home life. They certainly wouldn't have eaten with them at the same table. So this is a radical new proposal for the new church—not just mixing together but becoming *one new humanity*!

You can see the massive waves it made by following the story of Peter and Cornelius in Acts 10 where Peter is called to visit Cornelius's household and preach the gospel to the "unclean" gentiles. When Peter visits, Cornelius and his household convert and are welcomed into the church, but this is still pretty controversial. There were Jews who thought that gentiles shouldn't join the church unless they first converted to Judaism, which for men meant being circumcised, thereby placing themselves under obligation to follow all the laws God gave to Moses (Gal 5:3). So Peter was risking severe disapproval from his fellow Jewish Christians welcoming Cornelius and his family into the church *as gentiles*, without first requiring conversion to Judaism.

In the meantime, Paul, as a pious Jew and zealous Pharisee, is converted and anointed by God to become the apostle to the gentiles—to preach the gospel and plant churches among them. Not only was he called to a people who were most *un*like him, but it was revealed to him that the gentiles could become one with the Jews "in Christ" without having to conform to a Jewish identity. It's interesting that Paul actually had very little to do with Peter and the other apostles in the years after his conversion. He just got on with his mission. What we do know is that he was convinced that when gentiles became Christians they didn't have to follow Jewish law because the cross of Christ is enough for salvation. They could be gentiles *and* Christians. This tells us that we don't need to add anything more to the cross, follow any rules, or tick any boxes.

So when Peter lost his nerve and started giving in to the Judaizers (the people who wanted the gentiles to be circumcised) Paul rebuked him publicly at Antioch! You can read about this is in Galatians 2:11–21. Here you'll see that Peter had become fearful of those who belonged to the circumcision group. He started well with Cornelius and then backtracked. If you read Acts 15 as well, you'll see that thankfully Peter changed his mind back again after Paul rebuked him in public, and in the end he supports Paul in his view that gentiles shouldn't be circumcised. They stood together and opposed the circumcision group.

The fact that Peter got scared and gave in at one point over a central gospel issue shows you the strength of the pressure that was brought to bear on him. The picture we have here is of Peter to-ing and fro-ing depending on who was influencing him. Paul, in contrast, comes across as a man of principle who knew his own mind and stood up for the equal status of the gentiles come what may. Paul had extremely strong views and stuck to them. Many believe that it was because he was gripped with a vision of what it meant for human beings to be "in Christ" and the freedom that this brings and he refused to compromise on it.

BREAKING DOWN WALLS

In Ephesians, Paul describes the effect of the cross as bringing down the dividing wall of hostility leaving nothing separating Christians from one another on the grounds of some being superior and some inferior. When he talks about this "wall of hostility" he must have had in mind the literal dividing wall in the Temple that would have separated Jewish men from Jewish women, Jewish people from gentiles, and Jewish freedmen from slaves and the unclean. The free, Jewish men were near the top of the pile and got to go nearer to the center of the Temple. The priests got closer still to the inner sanctuary. Unclean men, women, and gentiles were kept further away with walls keeping them out from the inner sanctuary and separating them from the Jewish males.

Worship in Jesus' time was strictly segregated and to be a free, Jewish male would have meant occupying the position closest to God. What happened in the early church was that certain Jews had become Christians but had carried on maintaining that kind of segregation. It's hard to give up a place of privilege, especially if it means giving way to people we assume are inferior to us. The Jewish Christians struggled with this. The obvious answer was to make the gentiles like them, to secure their status. But we know how Paul reacted to segregation and to Christians who thought that they were superior to others. He thought it was directly contrary to the gospel. Here are two more examples.

SLAVES AND FREE

N. T. Wright, in his book *Paul and the Faithfulness of God*, spends the whole of the first chapter looking at how Paul understood the impact of the gospel on slaves and freedmen. He takes this from Paul's letter to Philemon. He makes the point that the main theme of this little letter is "reconciliation" between two men who are both Christians and so who are now brought into a relationship that is one of family—brothers. Wright describes this as a Messiah-and Spirit-driven unity.[1]

Onesimus was a slave who had run away from his master, Philemon. He ended up with Paul and had become a Christian. Paul clearly loved him but wanted him to go back and be reconciled with the master that he had run away from so he writes a

1. Wright, *Paul and the Faithfulness of God*, 9.

letter for Onesimus to take back to Philemon when he goes back home. Paul knows that he can't force Philemon not to punish Onesimus, but he makes it really clear that he thinks Philemon should treat Onesimus as his equal from now on. Paul tells Philemon that as they are now both "in the Lord" that he should take him back as a brother. Onesimus is a beloved "son" to Paul and so should be a beloved brother to Philemon.[2]

Wright writes, "The whole letter is both an expression of, and an exhortation to, the central Pauline theme of *koinonia*," which means "fellowship" or "partnership."[3] More than this though, Wright describes this little letter as evidence of Paul's "profoundly revolutionary" theology. It shows us that Paul is attempting to initiate a "social and cultural earthquake," or rather that he thinks this earthquake has already begun by "God's action in the Messiah."[4] It's radical theology with concrete implications. Philemon and Onesimus, master and slave, now have to worship together as equals and treat each other like brothers.

RICH AND POOR

Our last example of how Paul sees relationships taking shape "in the Lord" is in 1 Corinthians itself, just after the text that we've been studying, namely 1 Corinthians 11:17–34. In Graeco-Roman society the meal table was a place where everybody had their place depending on their wealth, importance, and social status. Rich people and men came first and were served first and everyone else was below them, going down the pecking order to the bottom. Sometimes rich wives had a place at the top with their husbands, but not always. And, as usual, the poor would come off worse.

In 1 Corinthians, Paul is angry with the Corinthians because poor people are going hungry at the communion table where others are stuffing themselves and getting drunk. The rich are

2. Ibid.

3. Ibid., 11.

4. Ibid., 9.

ignoring the poor. Paul is outraged. It's over this issue that he tells them that their meetings are doing more harm than good (11:17)! "[D]o you show contempt for the church of God and humiliate those who have nothing?" (11:22). Paul tells them instead to care for one another, especially those in need, "so then, my brothers and sisters, when you come together to eat, wait for one another" (11:33). Where the Corinthians are still maintaining social distinctions and segregation at the meal table, Paul warns them in no uncertain terms that these distinctions of superiority and inferiority based on worldly status have no place any more in the *Lord's* Supper.

THE "BODY" AT CORINTH

Paul uses the picture of a body to illustrate the values that he wants them to live by. He emphasizes their total unity and connection with Christ (as their head), complete unity with each other, the need for interdependence, care and honor of *all* members, and humility. He goes much farther though in turning their Roman and Greek values on their head. The strong are not just supposed to care for the weak, but to give them *greater* honor.

> [O]n the contrary, those parts of the body that seem to be weaker are indispensable, and the parts that we think are less honorable we clothe with greater honor. But God has so arranged the body, giving the greater honor to the inferior member, that there may be no dissension within the body, but the members may have the same care for one another. If one member suffers, all suffer together with it; if one member is honored, all rejoice together with it .... (12:22–25)

This applies to all—men and women, rich and poor, slave and free. Remember, as we saw in chapter 3, Christ is the head of the church so men and women all have one head. The church (all of us) is his body. This is the big picture of the church in 1 Corinthians. It's a body where the poor take their place equally with the rich at the Lord's Supper. More than that really, it's where the poor are *preferred* and the weak are honored. Hierarchy isn't just abolished; it's turned upside down!

If this is the vision that Paul had for the churches that he was leading, it makes me very much doubt that he thought women needed an extra sign on their heads to deal with any potential shame and to show that they are acceptable to God before they pray and prophesy. This idea doesn't seem to fit with Paul's passion that the church is a place where the gentiles don't have to conform to Jewish law and where the poor and people at the bottom of the pile in society are honored. There is more though. The church is also a place, according to Paul, where Christian values turn society's views of what is shameful and honoring on their head. This poses even more problems for us in imagining that Paul has had a sudden change of heart in 1 Corinthians 11.

SHAME AND HONOR

Remember that our passage, at its core, is about shame and honor. I think I've made the point clearly enough that the source of shame is not cultural but theological. So the shame is a "spiritual" shame and the honor is about honoring one another, God, Christ, and the angels with our behavior. It's not because of the shame/honor codes of the culture or because of what outsiders will think. Why might this be strange for Paul?

PAUL THE APOSTLE OF SHAME

The shame/honor motif certainly does run through the whole of 1 Corinthians, but in a way that completely opposes the idea that Christians should be concerned with their own shame and honor in society's eyes! In fact, it's even worse than that, because just *being* a Christian means that we will be shamed. Paul is fully aware that he has to face shame both in the world's eyes and in the church's eyes among his opponents. He has already faced that reality because of his commitment to the cross of Christ. He has given up any promise of kudos in any shape or form. The Corinthians, on the other hand, are obsessed with honor, strength, wisdom, and knowledge. They want as much as they can get. Paul mocks them for this. "We are fools for Christ, but you are so wise in Christ! We are weak, but you are strong! You are honored, but we are dishonored!" (1 Cor 4:10).

Paul knows that following Christ and apostleship is characterized by public dishonor and disgrace. "For it seems to me that God has put us apostles on display at the end of the procession, like men condemned to die in the arena. We have been made a spectacle to the whole universe, to angels as well as men" (1 Cor 4:9). Or in the ESV it reads, "For I think that God has exhibited us apostles as last of all, as though sentenced to death, because we have become a spectacle to the world, to angels and to mortals."

Paul here is saying that the angels *are* watching, but what they see is the true apostles mocked and scorned by the world in the public arena. Following Christ, for Paul, means being identified with the scum of the earth, literally, the scrapings from the bottom of a shoe (1 Cor 4:8–13). It's hard to emphasize enough how passionately Paul describes this. Not just this, but Paul claims that God chooses the foolish, the lowly, the weak and the despised *in order to shame* the wise, the strong, and the boastful (1 Cor 1:20–31).

I think it would be strange then for Paul suddenly to teach about *the lack of head coverings* as a sign of dishonor and disgrace. It wouldn't be odd for the Corinthians though.

THE CORINTHIAN OBSESSION WITH HONOR

Scholars will tell you that the Corinthians were steeped in a culture where everyone was concerned with shame and honor—how do we make sure we look good? Ben Witherington III writes, "The Corinthian people thus lived with an honor-shame cultural orientation, where public recognition was often more important than facts. . . . In such a culture a person's sense of worth is based on recognition by others of one's accomplishments."[5] They had an "obsessive concern to win reputation and status in the eyes of others."[6] How do you think Paul's teaching went down in a place like this?

Witherington writes, "In a city where social climbing was a major preoccupation, Paul's deliberate stepping down in apparent status would have been seen by many as disturbing, disgusting, and even provocative."[7] So it was *Paul* who was being "disturbing, disgusting and even provocative." Even more so, I imagine, because of his long hair!

John Barclay, another Pauline scholar, makes precisely the same point about people constantly being in the public eye in the ancient world and the need to show off their honor and glory. He describes honor as a "precious but unstable commodity."[8] You wanted to hold on to it, but you could easily lose it. And he goes on to talk about how glory was understood in the ancient world. A person's glory "needed to 'shine.'" It was "the object of perpetual surveillance."[9] People were always watching you to see if you could hold on to your honor and glory or whether you might fall from grace. So, apparently, it "was under the spotlight of communal attention that individuals would either display or damage their worth."[10] Imagine the anxiety around that. This sounds remarkably like the reason given for why men shouldn't wear head coverings doesn't it? But did Paul suffer from this anxiety? It sounds remarkably unlike Paul, who had given up all hope of saving face in the public eye.

5. Witherington, *Conflict and Community*, 21.

6. Ibid.

7. Ibid.

8. Barclay, *Paul and the Gift*, 434.

9. Ibid.

10. Ibid.

THE PUBLIC SHAME OF JESUS

I'm pretty sure that Paul didn't think that the glory of the Christian man would or should be recognized by everyone around him. Paul gave up every possibility of public recognition or honor because of his identification with Jesus Christ. Instead, in the letter to 1 Corinthians especially, we read that he identifies with the lowest of the low, and this is because he is identifying with his Savior and Master, who also gave up his glory and embraced public shame. I'm also pretty sure that he didn't think God had a hierarchy of glory and honor linked to what we wear or whether we display our hair.

What is especially fascinating for me is that Jesus was willing to be shamed and dishonored in public by *women*, much to the disgust of his disciples. There is a story, told in all four Gospels, of a prostitute or loose woman who gatecrashes a party to get close to Jesus. They must have met before because she needed to see him to thank him and honor him for all that he had done for her when he forgave her of her public sin and shame. What is so striking is that in her overwhelming gratitude she puts aside all thought of *his* shame and honor. She disgraces him terribly in public.

Uncovering a man's feet was an intimate and even sexual gesture, and totally inappropriate at this dinner party. Imagine this being done to Jesus in public by a known prostitute! She uncovers his feet, anoints them with oil, weeps over him, and then wipes his feet—*with her hair*.[11] This was an outrage, and the men around Jesus *were* outraged by it—not only by her, but by Jesus' acceptance of her lavish and disgraceful gesture. Who did she think she was and what was Jesus doing allowing this breach of cultural codes? What did Jesus mean by allowing her to do this? Jesus refuses to be criticized for this and instead rebukes his critics: "Truly I tell you, wherever this good news is proclaimed in the whole world, what she has done will be told, in remembrance of her" (Matt 26:6–13; Mark 14:3–9; Luke 7:36–47; John 12:1–8). The story is told, not in memory of the Savior, but in memory of *her*.

---

11. The connection between 1 Corinthians 11 and John 12:1–8 was first brought to my attention by Joel Mennie.

I'm left with these questions:

- Is it more likely that Paul or the Corinthians were most concerned with shame and honor and how things appear to society around them?

- Does what women wear truly act as a sign that will shield them from spiritual shame, not just in Paul's eyes, but supposedly, in God's eyes and because of the angels?

PAUL'S ATTITUDE TO WOMEN

We've looked at Paul's attitude to church as a place of reconciliation, the church as the body of Christ, and to his attitudes to shame and honor. In chapter 1, we described his relationships with countless women who had leadership positions in his churches. There has been a lot of work on this in recent years and many scholars now recognize that Paul worked closely with women on his mission, entrusting them with all and any tasks. The names I mentioned in chapter 1 of women who appear in Paul's letters give us evidence that Paul appointed or recognized women as prophets, leaders, teachers, and even apostles. I'm not going to repeat much of the work done by people on this here. If you are interested in exploring this issue, then I would recommend searching through Scot McKnight's blog, "The Jesus Creed," where you will find countless resources and book reviews on this issue.

We have to ask, did all these women wear head coverings whenever they ministered in church? If we think we're hearing Paul's voice in 1 Corinthians 11:2–16 then we would have to assume so. His parting shot to the Corinthians is that they should recognize his apostolic authority and do what he tells them, as he has "no such custom" in any of his churches. What custom is that? It is either the wearing of head coverings or the freedom from them. Whatever it is, it is one that he enforces in all his churches. As he never mentions the rule for women to wear head coverings anywhere else and we know that in other churches they were told not to ornament their hair extravagantly (so presumably their heads weren't covered),[12] we have very little evidence that this was a rule that Paul enforced everywhere in all his churches for all his women friends.

THE SCHOLARLY WORLD

I began by telling you that this is one of the most confusing and disputed passages in the New Testament—maybe even the whole Bible! You'll never find a bunch of scholars agreeing on everything, but there are some things that a large and significant group of contemporary Pauline scholars *are* agreed on, and that is how they see Paul's vision for a new humanity and consequently how that would have shaped his view of women. Even if they then admit that they can't really explain everything about some of the more difficult passages in Paul, they are all agreed that Paul's overall intent must have been to involve women in all his work at all levels. It's encouraging that so many male scholars have now come to this conclusion. I'll finish this chapter by giving you some examples of these top Pauline and New Testament scholars, and then you can always read them for yourself.

First, we looked at N. T. Wright and his view of Jew and gentile and slave and free as equals in worship. He follows this through in his belief in women in leadership in the church and you can read a bit about it in his book *Surprised by Scripture*. Douglas Campbell makes the point that we've been talking about above. Christian baptism creates a new form of human relations where the Christian's status of "sonship" overrules the normal categories that create difference within society, especially with regard to superior/inferior relations. He writes:

> (The Galatians are said, in the space of three verses, to be "in Christ" [and this twice], to be clothed "in" Christ, and to be immersed "into" Christ.) He [Paul] interprets this to mean that the Galatian Christians, irrespective of their previous positioning within the potentially diverse subcategories of present society, have been shifted into a

12. See 1 Tim 2:9; 1 Pet 3:3–4.

> mutually exclusive category of uniform sonship in Christ
> that displaces their previous existence, whatever it was—
> a dramatic set of claims![13]

Scot McKnight is convinced that the Bible frees women into all forms of ministry and leadership. He has a study in reading Scripture through different lenses in *The Blue Parakeet* and a little e-book on Junia the apostle and the way in which Bible translators had to come to the point where they admitted that Paul was referring to a female apostle.[14]

John Barclay has written a large book called *Paul and the Gift* in which he doesn't refer to Paul's views on women, but his work is of interest because he does write about Paul's conversion as a "profound dislocation" "which has wholly reconstituted his existence."[15] Barclay believes that Paul's communities were places where old values and systems of hierarchy, honor and shame, superiority and inferiority gave way to "communities freed from hierarchical systems of distinction . . . ."[16] His conclusion from his study of Galatians is that Paul is describing what this new Christian existence looks like in practical terms "in the freedom of common meals shared by Jews and non-Jews, in the creative operations of the Spirit, and in a communal ethos, grounded in baptism, that disregards normal criteria of honor and worth."[17] This view of Barclay's is hard to reconcile with a picture of Paul in Corinth telling the Corinthians that they weren't paying enough attention to a made-up rule that women should be covered.

Richard Hays admits that on the role of women in the social organization and worship life of the Pauline churches, "[t]he letters seem to send mixed signals."[18] It's difficult for Hays because he does believe that Paul thinks women should wear head coverings, and he also believes that Paul released women into leadership. So

---

13. Campbell, *The Quest*, 99–100.

14. See McKnight, *Junia Is Not Alone*.

15. Barclay, *Paul and the Gift*, 386.

16. Ibid., 397.

17. Ibid., 421–22.

18. Hays, *Moral Vision*, 1560.

he suggests that the best way to handle the stark tension that we find in the letters is to "examine the evidence concerning the roles *actually* played by women in the Pauline communities."[19] When he does this, this is what he finds,

> The cumulative weight of this evidence suggests that women did play a significant role in the ministry of the Pauline churches, including serving as members of the apostolic mission teams. Certainly, women participated in the activity of prophecy, which had as its purpose the upbuilding of the church (1 Cor 14:1–25). In many respects, women in these communities enjoyed a greater measure of freedom and dignity than they could have experienced in Greco-Roman society outside the Christian fellowship. Indeed, the relatively egalitarian social structure of the Pauline communities made them particularly attractive to "upwardly mobile" urban women whose education or economic position ("achieved status") exceeded their hereditary social position ("attributed status").[20]

And, finally, Philip Payne quite rightly emphasizes Paul's unusual affirmation of women. He notes that in "Col 2:10–11, Paul affirms that all Christians, female as well as male, 'have this fullness of the Godhead in Christ . . . in whom you were also circumcised.' Paul depicts females as having the fullness of the Godhead and being 'circumcised,' and he depicts males as members of the bride of Christ (Eph 5:22–27) because their gender is irrelevant to their being in the image of God and their being in Christ."[21] Further to this, Payne goes on to comment on Ephesians 2:14, not only in relation to Jew and gentile, but also to man and woman.

> Christ "has made the two one and has destroyed the barrier, the dividing wall of hostility" between Jew and Gentile. The court of the women with its own dividing wall lay between the court of the Gentiles and the temple.

19. Ibid., 1571.
20. Ibid., 1596.
21. Payne, *Man and Woman*, 69.

82

Galatians 3:28 implies the spiritual abolition of both of these walls and the consequent opening of temple-fellowship status to women as well as Gentiles. Similarly, the abolition of the necessity of circumcision (e.g., Eph 2:11–13) opens the door to full participation by women as well as Gentiles in Christian worship.[22]

WHAT ARE WE LEFT WITH?

We are left with various choices. We can choose to ignore the great weight of evidence that tells us Paul appointed women to all ministries in the early church and focus in on some verses that tell us what someone thought women should *not* do, pretending that these verses are uncomplicated and straightforward. There is a lack of honesty in this though, especially with our verses in 1 Corinthians 11:2–16, which contain some strange theology that is out of step with the rest of the Bible. Hays very honestly describes the views here as both "labored" and "unpersuasive theological arguments."[23] And he thinks this is Paul! So Hays is left admitting that he still thinks that Paul insists on the "maintenance of traditional markers of sexual distinction,"[24] even if it is based on some unpersuasive theological argument.

I'm still not persuaded that Paul felt so passionately about this strange theological picture that we have painted for us in 1 Corinthians 11:2–16. Some people think that Paul was just double-minded, or confused. Others think that he tried to hold two contradictory views at once or two views "in tension," even if that makes him incoherent. I don't believe that. I don't believe he misread Genesis or that he was worried about what people might think if they walked in and a woman was praying without a head covering or a man had long hair and had left his on! If we really take 1 Corinthians 11:3–10 at face value then we are faced with a distortion of the Christian truths and a strange view of the

22. Ibid., 93.

23. Hays, *Moral Vision*, 1645.

24. Ibid.

universe that has more in common with the Roman and Greek world that Paul was part of than his new Christian worldview. My view is that we can leave it at that, or we can find a better solution.

Conclusion

One of the purposes of this study guide is to demonstrate that anyone who thinks they can use these verses to "prove" that women need some sort of covering from a man to lead, minister, or serve in church is basing their argument on impossible grounds. There is no "proof." It is too convoluted and too conflicted a text to prove anything, and we should be able to admit this. We can show that if we take a traditional view of our passage (that Paul wrote it all and believed it all), then it's impossible to avoid a terrible theology of gender, or the conclusion that Paul is confused at times and double-minded at others. You could, of course, decide that, and that is one option.

If you study Paul, and especially Paul on women, you'll find that there are many differences in the views people have. There are both inconsistencies between the thinking of different readers and even in the thinking of individual scholars. There are people who claim that Paul's a brilliant letter writer and a genius of sorts, constructing his letters with great attention to detail and rhetoric. But if this is really so, did he just have a bad day with 1 Corinthians 11?

What about his commitment to women in all forms of ministry? We have evidence of that. If Paul did appoint women into all positions of leadership, did he just panic one day and take it all back? If Paul really believed that in Christ we are all one and that the dividing wall of hostility had been broken down, did he suddenly put one up again between men and women? Did he decide, on the one hand, that this theology of reconciliation would have a profound impact on the real relations of Jews and gentiles, slaves and free, and men and women, and then go back on it all in Corinth?

The truth is that the Bible doesn't present us with a uniform set of data from which to extrapolate one hard and fast rule, or a rigid protocol for men and women. In fact, we have a set of data that sometimes baffles us but invites us to dig deep and to explore more. It challenges us to think deeply and to question. This can be troubling and taxing at times, but it's worth the work. One thing that I am sure of is that it is time to stop imagining that the Bible prohibits the appointing of women as apostles, prophets, and teachers. This prohibition cannot be supported by the text that we have studied here in this book, and it cannot be supported by the bigger picture that we see in the New Testament. This means that we have to tackle the final difficult texts on women in a different way, but that is the subject for another book! For now, the burden of proof is on the other foot. The people who think that Paul really did prohibit women from full participation in the early church need to explain away the catalog of evidence that says he did not.

I have weighed up the evidence for myself and have opted for a reading of Paul that paints a consistent picture of Paul the apostle, Paul the man, Paul the friend of women, Paul the radical theologian, and Paul the visionary. I've chosen a reading that supports the view of Paul that you read of in the works of N. T. Wright, John Barclay, Scot McKnight, Michael Gorman, Philip Payne, Gordon Fee, Ben Witherington III, R. T. France, and many others.

I came to the conclusion that Paul was faced with a group of domineering, gifted, prophetic men who had implemented oppressive practices for women in Paul's absence. They constructed a theology to support their practices that was a blend of Paul's original thought and their own distorted view of the world. Paul addresses this issue, citing their letter to him and correcting them. Bruce Winter, another Pauline scholar, describes perfectly for me what I think had happened. He believes that the Corinthian church had lost sight of Paul's teachings after he left Corinth, and had fallen prey to the influence of secular ethics or social conventions. "They may have crept into the church imperceptibly and grown with the passage of time."[1] He believes Paul was addressing a specifically masculine culture of dominance, competitiveness, rivalry, and divisiveness that was more like the Roman culture of the day than it was like the Christ-like leadership Paul had modeled for them. We know that there were a group of men in the church behaving "like other men do" (1 Cor 3:3), i.e., like the secular Romans behaved with one another, with jealousy, quarrelling, and rivalry.

This is why I imagine the church at Corinth as I do. The Corinthian church was being dominated by a group of spiritually gifted and highly articulate teachers who were both overbearing and divisive men. It was they who believed, among other things, and partially from a version of Paul's teaching in the first place, that men and women should display signs of their own status before God, one another, and the angels in worship. Because, according to Genesis 2, women were created second, the Corinthians were teaching that they have a secondary place in the creation order, deriving their glory not directly from Christ, but from man. For this reason, they needed to wear a sign of authority/subjection/honor on their "heads." As man is the glory of Christ, and Christ is the "head" of man, however, men must display this glory by remaining bareheaded.

I imagine that these men could have been both powerful and forceful, pronouncing the "Word of God," laying down the law, and arguing that if a woman was bareheaded this was tantamount to appearing before God as a prostitute and thus shaming the men, the angels, and God himself. She may as well appear shaven. They may even have articulated this in their letter to Paul. These Corinthian men were more concerned about their shame and honor than the cross of Christ, and they were forceful and gifted enough to have imposed their will. Not only is this, sadly, so easy to imagine given what we know of the church, my reading makes sense of the passage in a way that others can't.

My conclusion is that I think that Paul is saying the *exact opposite* of what most people think he says. If we accept this reading,

1. Winter, *After Paul*, 4.

it turns the situation on its head. It means that Paul begins and ends his section on public worship by addressing the oppression, suppression and silencing of women, and coming out as strongly as possible against it.

Bibliography

Augustine. *De Trinitate*. Edited by Edmund Hill. New York: New City, 1991.

Barclay, John M. G. *Paul and the Gift*. Grand Rapids: Eerdmans, 2015.

Bilezikian, Gilbert. *Beyond Sex Roles: What the Bible Says about a Woman's Place in Church and Family*. Grand Rapids: Baker Academic, 2006.

Bushnell, Katherine C. *God's Word to Women: One Hundred Bible Studies on Women's Place in the Divine Economy*. Oakland, CA: Katharine C. Bushnell, 1923. Reprint. Peoria, IL: Jolliff and Menold, n.d.

Campbell, Douglas A. *The Deliverance of God: An Apocalyptic Rereading of Justification in Paul*. Grand Rapids: Eerdmans, 2009.

————. *The Quest for Paul's Gospel: A Suggested Strategy*. London: T. & T. Clark, 2005.

Chrysostom, John. *Homilies on the Epistles of Paul to the Corinthians*. Nicene and Post-Nicene Fathers, Series 1, Vol. 14. Edited by Philip Schaff. Edinburgh: T. & T. Clark, 1889.

France, R. T. *Women in the Church's Ministry: A Test Case for Biblical Interpretation*. Grand Rapids: Eerdmans, 1995.

Hays, Richard B. *The Moral Vision of the New Testament: Community, Cross, New Creation. A Contemporary Introduction to New Testament Ethics*. New York: HarperCollins e-books, 2013.

Holmes, Steve. "John Chrysostom on 1 Cor. 11:3." Shored Fragments. http://steverholmes.org.uk/blog/?p=7510 (accessed Dec 31, 2015).

Lakey, Michael J. *Image and Glory of God: 1 Corinthians 11:2–16 as a Case Study in Bible, Gender and Hermeneutics*. London: T. & T. Clark, 2010.

McKnight, Scot. *The Blue Parakeet: Rethinking How You Read the Bible*. Grand Rapids: Zondervan. 2008.

————. *Junia Is Not Alone: Breaking Our Silence about Women in the Bible and the Church Today*. Englewood, CO: Patheos, 2011.

Padgett, Alan G. *As Christ Submits to the Church: A Biblical Understanding of Leadership and Mutual Submission*. Grand Rapids: Baker Academic, 2011.

Payne, Philip B. *Man and Woman, One in Christ: An Exegetical and Theological Study of Paul's Letters*. Grand Rapids: Zondervan, 2009.

————. "Wild Hair and Gender Equality in 1 Corinthians 11:2–16." *Priscilla Papers* 20.3 (2006) 9–18.

Peppiatt, Lucy. *Women at Worship at Corinth: Paul's Rhetorical Arguments in 1 Corinthians 11–14.* Eugene, OR: Wipf and Stock, 2015.

Shoemaker, Thomas P. "Unveiling of Equality: 1 Corinthians 11:2–16." *Biblical Theology Bulletin* 17 (1987) 60–63.

Vadakkedom, Jose. "The Letter of Corinthians to Paul the Apostle." *Bible Bhashayam* 34.4 (2008) 273–97.

Winter, Bruce W. *After Paul Left Corinth: The Influence of Secular Ethics and Social Change.* Grand Rapids: Eerdmans, 2001.

Witherington III, Ben. *Conflict and Community in Corinth: A Socio-Rhetorical Commentary on 1 and 2 Corinthians.* Grand Rapids: Eerdmans, 1995.

Wright, N. T. *Colossians and Philemon.* Leicester, UK: IVP, 1986.

————. *Paul and the Faithfulness of God.* 2 vols. London: SPCK, 2013.

————. *Surprised by Scripture: Engaging Contemporary Issues.* NY: HarperOne, 2015.

Lightning Source UK Ltd.
Milton Keynes UK
UKOW01f0344100218
317653UK00001B/106/P